LETTERS
FROM BARON FRIEDRICH
VON HÜGEL TO A NIECE

Edited with an Introduction by

GWENDOLEN GREENE

LONDON

J. M. DENT & SONS LTD.

NEW YORK: E. P. DUTTON & Co. INC.

All rights reserved
Made in Great Britain
at the
Aldine Press · Letchworth · Herts
for
J. M. DENT & SONS LTD
Aldine House · Bedford Street · London
First published 1928
Last reprinted 1965

Le monde voit en elle les passions, l'intérêt, l'ambition; il voit l'eau amère qui remplit les choses; et nous, nous cherchons sous les eaux amères cette petite source Aréthuse qui continue sa course, cette petite suite de la grâce, plus profonde, plus cachée, mais qui existe pourtant.

ABBÉ HUVELIN, *Quelques Directeurs d'Ames.*

I know that thou canst do every thing . . . Therefore have I uttered that I understood not; things too wonderful for me, which I knew not. . . . I have heard of thee by the hearing of the ear: but now mine eye seeth thee.

Job xlii.

Through such souls alone
God stooping shows sufficient of His light
For us i' the dark to rise by.
And I rise.

ROBERT BROWNING, "Pompilia," *The Ring and the Book.*

FOREWORD

MORE perhaps to-day than ever before, the man who looks for guidance in resolving the enigma of human existence demands that his would-be guide shall speak with an utterly sincere conviction clearly based on the deepest personal experience and knowledge of realities underlying deceptive and unsatisfying appearances. Is it cynical to say that many a spokesman for Christianity, however real to him his own faith, suggests that he is only passing on a formula—an answer, as it were, from the last pages of a book of puzzles—not the fruits of his own spiritual and intellectual grappling with life? On the other hand, should he convey this sense of personal experiment and struggle, how often do his discoveries seem bare, one-sided, and insufficient!

Friedrich von Hügel, more than any religious thinker of recent times, succeeded in impressing those who met or read him with that personal, utterly sincere, splendidly courageous living of the whole Christian way which alone can fully convince the seeker after truth, whether he be a conventional Christian or no Christian at all.

Born into the Catholic Church nearly a hundred years ago, his father an Austrian diplomat and his mother a Scotswoman, he devoted his whole life, lived in England, to what in fact was a kind of scholar's examination into the authenticity of Catholic Christianity as God's full revelation to man. In this life-quest, he avoided the two commonest errors of such an enterprise.

He did not attempt to judge of Christianity from outside Christianity, as though a man without an ear for music or an eye for painting were to judge the worth of these arts; neither did he take his faith for granted, and then find ingenious reasons to persuade others of its validity, as when a man having been told the answer to a mathematical sum works backward to discover the way to solve it. What he did was to live the Christian faith, as few have done, testing, inquiring, experimenting at every turn, and never subscribing to a judgment or formula until he had seen its truth for himself, fitting it into the great pattern whose grandeur is only revealed as it is thus traced in life, research, and prayer.

It was characteristic of him that his first book was published at the age of fifty-six. Inevitably much of the work of such a man makes tough reading. But in his old age he was able more freely and easily to find ways of expressing and conveying something of his life of spiritual discovery. Some of his essays and many of his letters are well within the compass of the ordinary reader. This was especially the case when he indulged one of his most charming characteristics. The old saint, for all his learning, always retained the personal simplicity of a child, and there was nothing he loved better than teaching and guiding children, who loved his funny stories and expressions, and were moved with wonder by his immense sincerity.

These Letters to a Niece were not written to a child, but, as Gwendolen Greene so beautifully explains in her Introduction, it was in the spirit of an old uncle dealing with a young niece that he guided her by word of mouth and by letter. That Introduction will convey something of their personal intercourse, the Letters

Foreword

themselves much of his advice. The two together make a wonderful initiation into the spiritual secrets of one who has been described as "the greatest religious thinker after Newman."

Our western world to-day, hardly able to find the way of recovery from the shock of the two great wars which shattered the dreams of an unchecked post-Christian progress and face to face with the aggression of a Godless totalitarianism, needs, as never before, to recover the lost treasure of man's spiritual destiny. I believe that few are more competent to help us all than this prophet of our own times, Friedrich von Hügel, the twenty-fifth anniversary of whose death occurs in this year of grace, 1950.

MICHAEL DE LA BEDOYÈRE.

INTRODUCTION

SOME of these letters have been published already in the *Selected Letters of Friedrich von Hügel*, others have not yet appeared in print. They are now collected and issued separately for those people to whom the larger book may be a difficulty—the people who are not interested in the more directly philosophical and theological sides of religion. Perhaps they have not the capacity, or the training; their way is more humble and they want to learn. They are like the simple people in the old hymn who say:

> I thirst for springs of heavenly life,
> And here all day they rise;
> I seek the treasure of Thy love,
> And close at hand it lies.[1]

They can say "I seek," but they do not know how to find; they hardly think that they *can* find. For to them religion is like the jewel in the toad's head—it is a fable—something unreal and apart from life. God if he exists is too far away, he might as well not be there at all; and Christ and the Saints belong to another age. Living realities once, startling and filling their world, they have no significance now, and hardly enter our thoughts. Ages ago they lived and died, suffered and were adored. Those things are not now, and no living soul can inhabit a church.

For many life becomes half-toned and pointless:

[1] From "My heart is resting, O my God."—*Anna Waring*.

all that they do disappointing and dim. The deepest things have lost their dignity, there is no value in anything in life. Their little bits of faith, of hope and love are fruitless, all disconnected like the beads of a broken necklace that lie scattered over the ground. There seems no way to connect them, no power to make them of worth. But my uncle knows how to connect them, he produces what restores them to life. He gathers these beads together with untiring love and care. He patiently searches and gathers them from wherever they may lie hidden, and he threads them on to their proper chain, the chain that unites us to God. For out of all our doings and cares, our hopes and fears, and loves, he makes a little home where the Spirit of Christ can dwell, and where, united to God by prayer, our souls can live and expand.

He "preaches Jesus." And when he tells us of God his face is lit and illumined by some interior fire. He speaks like a prophet. He burns with his message— what he sees, he makes us see. As before some tremendous catastrophe, some sublime grief or love, we are drawn into an awe and a worship of God we can never escape or forget.

When he speaks of Our Lord and his Church and the Saints, he reveals these for us. They emerge as realities—greater than any, obliterating all we have known. They obliterate all—yes—but only to renew, re-create, and instil in our souls that love that he knows: a love deeper and closer than any, within and without us, enfolding, inspiring our lives.

"To sanctify is the biggest thing out." These words of his ring in my mind. They express what he was,

what he meant, what he wished most to do. His whole
life lies in them. He tried to find truth, to teach us
God, to sanctify our lives. He loved, and he wanted
to teach us to love. Can one soul communicate love
to another?

I am adding to these letters the conversations that
I had with my uncle during the same period of time.
(Much, I am afraid, has been forgotten, though the
impression remains.) They express the same desire,
they have the same aim. He wanted, as he says somewhere, to train me "in faith, trust and love of God,
Christ and the Church." They help fill in to some
extent the picture that I would like to give of him.
It is a double picture, a picture of him teaching, and
a picture of what he taught.

He told me often, how one trained soul could teach
another, one soul radiate light to another soul, one
saint make another saint. "That is the great tradition—I never learnt anything myself by my own
old nose." So here we can try, through these letters and talks, to learn what he learnt; and to love
and to follow the way that he loved and lived for
so many years.

I cannot attempt to describe my uncle. Many can
do that so much better than I. I am dominated and
absorbed by his greatness. He seems to me as rich
and large as the world. I am lost in his depth, silenced
by his nobility. I remember his words to me about
great things: "Be silent about great things; let them
grow inside you. Never discuss them: discussion is so
limiting and distracting. It makes things grow smaller.
You think you swallow things when they ought to

swallow you. Before all greatness, be silent—in art, in music, in religion: silence." And so before him I must be silent, and let him speak for himself.

"I want to make the most of whatever light people have got, however slight it may be, to strengthen and deepen whatever they already possess, if I can." He dreaded to strain or complicate people, to mix up their "attraits" for them.

[margin note: making what light is there]

"Leave out all that does not help you. Take only what you can, and what helps. Wipe your feet on my old hair, if it will help you, my little old thing," was one of his first injunctions to me. And "Our Lord tells us not to put out the smoking flax, not to break the bruised reed—and yet I always see *this*. God makes lovely little flowers grow everywhere, but some-one always comes and sits on them." He could not help it if people were impressed by his way, and his mind, but he never wanted to make people grow into his own mould.

[margin note: consideration of little people]

When I look at the notes of his talks (very fragmen-tary, and only made after they occurred) I am bewil-dered by the amount of things he talked about. Discriminations on people, things, books, histories, movements, besides actual religion and direction of life. He touched on nearly everything, and it is impossible to publish all this here: I am obliged to make a selection. Then there are all his jokes and stories, his most curious adjectives and slang words; so peculiarly suitable to the things and people he describes, and so extremely characteristic—one loves them almost best of all.

How well I remember the "whole-hoggers" and the "lumpers," the "meansters" and "fusty" people,

[margin note: people he disliked]

whom he could not stand; and the people who asked
him the same question thirty times. "I cannot make
them out at all," he used to say with a very bewildered
face. "They are like flying beetles, first they bump
into your eye, then into your boot." The people whose
minds were like slop-basins and those "who water
broomsticks to grow roses" tried him very much; and
lastly he used to speak wistfully of those "who can't
swallow one potato, but try to swallow eight!" "My
old boot" was a very favourite expression. "Rashdall
has as much mysticism in him as my old boot."
Throwing his old boot, or both his old boots, or "all
my old boots" at the young Anglican clergy seemed
one of his most favourite pastimes. He used to laugh
tremendously over his own jokes.

It was not till 1919 that he began his regular talks
with me. I sat beside him, always on the same little
low chair (just as we always had to keep to the same
day, if possible—it had some tremendous significance!).
I always felt like a child with my uncle, and I never
attempted to be anything else. As he said, I had to
learn, and I am still in a spiritual childhood. Everything was carefully prepared before my arrival. He
liked me best to knit while I listened. He said
people always listened best when they did something with their hands, more especially women.
His plan was all thought out : he wanted to try
and strengthen my character, feed my soul : and
I was to learn through history, as well as through
religion itself. "I want to prepare you, to organise
you for life, for illness, crisis, and death"; and the
essence of his first as of his last talk might be said in
his own words: "Live all you can—as complete and

full a life as you can find—do as much as you can for others. Read, work, enjoy—love and help as many souls—do all this. Yes—but remember: Be alone, be remote, be away from the world, be desolate. Then you will be near God!"

I must often have disappointed him. He was so humble, he thought everyone could remember, understand, and discriminate, as he did himself. But if he was disappointed, he never showed it. He went on with his teaching with a beaming face. He said it was clearly my duty to read—"to do a great amount of reading, *not* to become a learned woman. A learned woman is an abomination, there is nothing to be done but to drown her. No—*not* to be a spectacled blue-stocking, but to be a deeply spiritual woman. I want to feed your mind and soul; to make you a sober, persevering, balanced, genial, historical Christian."

So we began by reading history, pagan history, and first of all Boissier's *Histoire du Paganisme*, then more Boissiers; then Cæsar, Cicero, Lucretius, Virgil, Tacitus, Horace, Livy, Pliny, Herodotus, Hesiod, Thucydides. The parcels came regularly, like books from a library, all carefully selected and chosen to suit my state, and always accompanied by a letter explaining their particular value or beauty. When we at last reached Christian things, we began with St. Augustine (which he read aloud to me, the most wonderful reading, in the garden at Clonboy, Englefield Green); the martyrs, Tertullian ("that great fierce African genius"), Jerome, *The Fathers in the Desert*, Minucius Felix, etc. Many were presents, selected translations, because I could not read Latin. When we got to Greek books, Plato, Aristotle, Plotinus, he gave me also guide-books on Greek statuary, and books on coins in the British Museum.

How I wish I could have it all over again, for perhaps I should understand and remember a little more! We were just starting on Indian religions with Farquhar's *Crown of Hinduism* at the time of his death. We went through all the English poets, from Cædmon to Browning. He loved Browning very much, and used to read him too aloud to me in the garden at Clonboy. But he was always distressed at Browning's appearing to think it was almost a necessity to commit some great sin in order to become ultimately a saint. "That's all wrong. I don't like that. We are not all St. Augustines. We should stay down in the mud and the mire. Even St. Augustine would have been a greater saint had he been innocent: magnificent, the Church canonising him!"

He never gave me any purely clever books; he could not bear them. "We never really get anything that way. Clever people never think. They are incapable of thinking—I have always found this so. Cleverness never goes with depth and real thinking." I never can forget his indignation when someone wanted me to read Locke and Hume. "Why should you, a living woman, read Locke or Hume? Can grammar alone feed the human soul? Locke is a dreary old man; he may have a God, but he is a dusty dim God. And Hume is blasé. He is the sort of person young people are taken in by: they take him for something else. He knows everything. He got to the bottom of everything by the time he was sixteen: he sees everything through clear glass windows. If I were to die to-night, he would know all about me by to-morrow. These old bones would be all arranged, sorted out, explained and in his coat-pocket; but somehow he would not have got me all the same." He never gave me any directly mystical books, except Mother Julian and Fr. Baker, both of whom he loved much.

In the earliest notes I made he speaks a great deal of the need to know history — not only religious history—but all history, especially for a religious woman. "A religious woman is often so tiresome, so unbalanced and excessive. She bores everyone, she has no historical sense. I want to teach you through history. History is an enlargement of personal experience, history pressing the past. We must have the closest contact with the past. How poor and thin a thing is all purely personal religion! Is there any such thing as a purely original thinker? You must get a larger experience—you gain it by a study of history; the individualistic basis simply doesn't work.

"I hate all the notion that there is no value in anything that is past—that the only value is in what we have got now. That cuts us right off, it gives us no base, it leaves out the richness and soundness of the great traditions. I want to teach you through all those gigantic things, the martyrs, gnosticism, scepticism, that atrocious thing the eighteenth century. I want you to learn about the great souls that lived through all those tracts of time. You will learn about progress. People talk so much about progress nowadays. Where is all this wonderful progress in the human soul? Religion to be deep and rich must be historical. I can't help it if you don't believe in religion, it's an historical fact. It is to demonstrate

and to explain its growth that Tiele wrote—the book
you liked so much.[1] Tiele's style is not elegant polished
English, but he is full of stuff. It is the *stuff* of religion
that matters. We will not idolise form; it is the richness of the content that counts. The New Testament
—what is it in form? It is nothing—it is not even
literature—but it is the bread of life. About knowledge
—so many people want to know, in order to know,
and nothing else. How empty all that is! What a
difference in Christianity!

"Christianity is a thing of the heart, and it's that
that matters. No other knowledge counts but that
that feeds and strengthens the mind and soul. The
spiritual world is a great world of facts, and you must
learn about it, as you would learn forestry from the
forester. After five or six years among the trees you
will know something about them. You are a goose if
you cavil at that! I learnt all that I know from
Huvelin. What I teach you is him, not me. I learnt
it from him. What a great saint he was! and what
he taught me! 'One torch lights another torch'
(Lucretius). One penitent soul awakens to the desire
to teach other souls—in sufferings and dryness a more
experienced soul can sustain the less. It is best to
learn from others; it gives a touch of creatureliness.
I don't know if that is a real word or not, but it is
almost my favourite adjective. Your ultimate light
is your own; but in the meantime you have got
to learn.

"Suffering is the greatest teacher; the consecrated
suffering of one soul teaches another. I think we have
got all our values wrong, and suffering is the crown

[1] Tiele, *Scientific History of Religion.*

of life. Suffering and expansion, what a rich combination!

"Religion has never made me happy; it's no use
shutting your eyes to the fact that the deeper you go,
the more alone you will find yourself. Suffering can
expand, it can contract. *La souffrance noble, la souffrance
basse.* Grasp the nettle, my little old thing! Religion
has never made me comfy. I have been in the deserts
ten years. All deepened life is deepened suffering,
deepened dreariness, deepened joy. Suffering and joy.
The final note of religion is joy.

"Do not be greedy of consolation. I never got
anything that way. Suffering teaches: life teaches.
Don't weaken love; never violate it. Love and joy
are your way. Be very humble, it's the only thing.
That is why I try to keep my little thing always on
her knees.

"Dullness, dreariness and loneliness. East winds
always blowing; desolation, with certain lucid intervals and dim assurances. Be always faithful. You
will find you would rather lose life itself than this
life. *Après tout*, the last act in life is devotion—devotion
in death. I like that.

"Religion is dim—in the religious temper there
should be a great simplicity, and a certain content-
ment in dimness. It is a great gift of God to have
this temper. God does not make our lives all ship-
shape, clear and comfortable. Never try to get things
too clear. Religion can't be clear. In this mixed-up
life there is always an element of unclearness. I believe
God wills it so. There is always an element of tragedy.
How can it be otherwise if Christianity is our ideal?
When I was a young man I was always interested in

religion, in the facts of religion, and I felt these facts
to be outside of myself, not my imagination. As far
as I can see them, they are quite beyond my imagination. If I could understand religion as I understand
that two and two make four, it would not be worth
understanding. Religion can't be clear if it is worth
having. To me, if I can see things through and through,
I get uneasy—I feel it's a fake. I know I have left
something out, I've made some mistake.

"You want to be truthful to find the truth, to be
truthful to find God. We can't eliminate all difficulties.
Some people don't want the truth. They get in the
train, but they won't go all the way: they get out in
a potato-field. These people make scepticism; they so-
phisticate the mind. We are like sponges trying to mop
up the ocean. We can never know God exhaustively.
God is simultaneous, *totum simul*: we are passing. How
splendidly the Roman Church has got that — the
time-limited and the timeless! We can never picture
God or imagine him. Either we make him too small,
and we strain at that, or we make him too big, and
he strains us. Let us rest content. We have not got to
invent God, nor to hold him. He holds us. We shall
never be able to explain God, though we can apprehend him, more and more through the spiritual life.
I want you to hold very clearly the *otherness* of God,
and the littleness of men. If you don't get that you
can't have adoration, and you cannot have religion
without adoration.

"I can't bear those people who talk about God
and us as mutualities. God and us little men! Man
the centre, and God coming to himself through us
men! I know more and more how small I am, how

great God is. He works *in* us, not by us. We shall never be God, we shall always be men. He gives: we receive. The given-ness of God—everything is given. The moderns say: 'Thank goodness we have got rid of the awful position of servant and master' (is it awful?). God needs us, as much as we need him. Canon S——— says God needs us to make the world. I must say I never heard Canon S—— helped God to make Saturn's rings! It sounds rather fusty somehow to me.

"How vulgar the eighteenth century was: a purely *this*-world affair. God and the other world went out completely. But though you can throw God out of man's life, he always manages to get back again. Man is both of, and not of, this world; the soul lives in two worlds—hence the tension. How splendidly Kant saw that! God is the great reality that penetrates our lives: the practice and presence of God—there, get that.

"Some people are so fond of ideas. A new idea is a kind of magic to them! I don't care about ideas, I want facts. God is not an idea. He is a fact. 'I find God outside of myself. He is an illapse from outside.' There, that is right, that does away with all this miserable subjectivism. I don't much like all this Coué business, all this dwelling on ourselves. Leave ourselves—let in God. I always think it is much harder for a healthy person to be really religious, to find God. When your body is a constant failure you cannot depend on yourself at all, so you turn to God. If you love God, and hate yourself, that's all right. We are becoming creatures—becoming in order to be—God *is*. We are getting to being. Religion is not man-made: it is immense: it comes from outside. Man rather spoils it, but in spite of all he can do, it remains immortal. The supernatural life is a life of renunciation. If we are Christians there are always two notes, suffering and joy. Gethsemane is awful, but it does not end with Gethsemane; there is the Resurrection. We want the *whole* of religion; renunciation and joy, the Cross and the Crown. I don't like Christians who have concentrated only on the Cross: Christianity is the *whole* life of Christ. His life of mortification, of suffering and sacrifice, culminating, it is true, in the Cross. But I can't bear the obliterating of his life, that great life lived, the touching humility and love. And the parables—look at the inexhaustible wonder of the parables, how beautiful they are! I like a balanced Christianity: Christianity *is* so balanced.

"What a wretched affair the eighteenth century! I often think of Herbert Spencer, picking up and reading Plato at the Club. His surprised, contemptuous admiration.[1] Spencer was a flea or a bug compared to Plato. The eighteenth-century ideal was the smug, comfy, utterly material domestic life. Is that the final end of man in Christianity? the decent, comfortable married man? No. No. Christianity is not that. The whole world would reject that: no primitive Christian would look at it for a moment. *Christianity is a heroism.* People seem sometimes to think it is a dear darling, not-to-be-grumpy, not-to-be-impatient, not-to-be-violent life; a sort of wishy-washy sentimental affair. Stuff and nonsense! Christianity is not that. Christianity is an immense warning; a tremendous

[1] Spencer was, of course, nineteenth-century, but perhaps my uncle meant he was a type of the eighteenth-century spirit.

heroism. Christ teaches a great austerity. He teaches renunciation: the life of the Cross. He was not comfy. He had not where to lay his head. He was no rigorist, yet he tells us to die to ourselves, to take up the Cross, to follow him. Is that all comfy? Christianity is coming back to renunciation, and to a right asceticism and austerity. That is what Our Lord teaches. If you don't see *that* in the Gospels, I don't see what you see.

"It's like fear. Fear went out altogether. It was an invention of priests. 'Perfect love casteth out fear.' But does it? You cannot build on one text like that. In all love there is an element of fear; an unabashed human being is a horrible thing. Fear is not always servile. Awe and reverence, they are fear purified and spiritualised. Fear is inseparable from love. That's jolly. Fear spiritualised is in all adoration. Religion without adoration is like a triangle with one side left out.

"I hope you will never become scrupulous. It is a bad thing all round, a morbid conscientiousness and brooding. Never brood, brooding is a waste of growth. How I have found this myself! It puts back all my work if I brood. Die without a breath of grievance: religion makes this possible, men have less the spirit of grievance.

"Drop things; always keep on dropping and dropping. My religion, my illness, suffering and life have taught me that. Always drop things. Don't chatter to yourself—you can't hear God if you do. We need not try to conceive God: he attends to all that. We have to make room for him in our souls. There was no room for Our Lord, you remember, at the inn. In this world, too, there is no room for him. Drop, then, all these things, these miseries: not by straining, or making or getting strength; but genially, gently; while attending, as you must, to these things, drop them; these flies that bother your nose, God nowhere visible. Resign yourself. That is God's plan —faithfully, wisely, resign yourself. Fussiness and activity! What a difference there is between action and activity (Aristotle, God is action)! People waste their lives in these countless little activities and fussinesses. When I get up feeling I have a hundred things to do—then I know it's all wrong. I try to get away, to go for a walk with Puck. I leave everything till I am better. I would like you to learn from St. Catherine of Genoa the point of always attending to but one thing at a time. This one action or suffering, joy or renunciation, being at that moment the *one* will of God and the one means of pleasing him and of attaining true growth in oneself. It is the *trait d'union* with God. The more full and varied your life becomes, the more this great principle and practice is necessary—to prevent distraction and racket. Goethe's mother, when she was dying, sent down a message to a caller that she could not see her as she was occupied in dying. 'I am busy with death.' That's right—so I hope too to turn to death, busy with that, one thing at a time. My own experience now when my life is twenty times as full as it was at eighteen, yet it is much more unified and recollected. The great rule is, *Variety up to the verge of dissipation: Recollection up to the verge of emptiness*: each alternating with the other and making a rich fruitful tension. Thus we gather honey from all sorts of flowers, then sort out,

arrange, unify and store, the honey gathered. After
which we again fly out on our honey-gathering expe-
ditions. What an immense activity was Fénelon's: and
a still larger activity St. Augustine's! Yet both were
deeply recollected men.

"Young people seem absorbed nowadays in getting
their own way. Matthew Arnold says you can get so
absorbed in heroism that *that* becomes your own way.
But you can't have growth if you do what you like as
we ordinarily mean it, until we come again to live
for duty and not for rights, to be busy with contrition
for sin and not with comforts. God is in duty. The
notion of being comfortable! How vulgar it is! God
never makes our lives comfortable. Even in heaven
I believe there will be an equivalent of suffering—
not as it stands here—but the equivalent, suffering
beatified. I feel sure of this.

Protestantism

"How curiously uncertain and uncomfortable people
are in Protestantism! It is the Calvinism in it, the
curious betwixt - and - between - ness. Protestants are
pledged to two mutually contradictory movements.
The reforming spirit of Erasmus and More was
splendid—but the strongly Calvinistic Protestant spirit
is so narrow and thin.

"The suppression and illegality of the crucifix in
England is the result of Calvinism. It is like image-
breaking. Preposterous! There is nothing more beautiful than the crucifix. Luther had no objection to
the crucifix—the Lutheran dies with it in his hand.
The cross is Protestant, and the crucifix Roman. The
Protestant Church contains in Anglicanism many
precious commitments of Catholicism, but it is a
compromise between Calvinism and Calvinism's *bête*

noire—the Roman Catholic Church. I love the Book
of Common Prayer—all except the Homilies and the
Thirty-nine Articles. I would like to wring the necks
of both of those.

"I hate rigorism—it's all wrong. Our Lord was never
a rigorist. He loved publicans and sinners. How he
loved all the beauties of nature, the family—children!
His parables are full of these homely things. God
nearly always teaches us through a person, he teaches
us through individuals. Follow his lead. Live from
day to day, even from hour to hour. I want you to
learn to die to yourself daily; the daily death is a
spiritual habit. You want heroism and renunciation
—more, you want wisdom and discipline: organise
yourself. Perseverance is one of the crowning graces
of God. Get rid of all self-occupation. I don't mean
self-examination for conscience' sake, though that,
too, can be overdone. But self-oblivion is a splendid
thing; move out of yourself, let in God. Never pray
but you realise that you are but one of a countless
number of souls, a countless number of stars.

"Do not suppress pleasures, but let them flop.
Pleasure is like the fringe of your dress, the afterness
of an act. Ignore them, let them flop, never work
directly for them.

"God always gives joy, even in spiritual things
there is a concomitant pleasure. There is a great
joy in renunciation. I just love the monkish conception,
it is the protest against the too much caring for the
world. There are two poles within the Church—the
heroic monastic, and the homely domestic pole. The
pole of renouncing—the monk; and the domestic pole
—the married people who go whole into things. We

need them both to make Christianity and the Church very wide, very deep and inclusive. The Roman Catholic Church proclaims them both as necessities, and both from God. She has never let go the monk —without him, what an impoverishment! When I was young and tempted to fall into sin, no old woman with a tract could have saved me. But I came across a Dominican monk. What a splendid man he was! What I learnt from him! He saved me from sin. I remember he said to me once, 'You think I do all this for pleasure? for show? Give up marriage, live in discomfort and cold, eat fish all the year round, that I do it to please myself? I don't, I hate it, but I do it for God. I do it to keep alive in this world the spirit that the world forgets—the spirit of renunciation, sacrifice, the supernatural life.' The body is the servant of the spirit. I think of Huvelin; look at him! What a great saint he was! What tremendous mortifications he went in for! All saints are excessive to start. He was a man of tremendous passion, tremendous intensity. And what wonderful gentleness and moderation he attained to! What patience! All that was the result of his self-discipline and excessive—yes, no doubt— excessive mortifications. No doubt he ruined his health — but what would you have? He did not despise passion, he sacrificed it, and he became a saint. No man was more tolerant of others; always suffering and ill, he sat in a chair radiating joy and support to all of us.

"Religion is not based on miracles. Put them on one side. They are often symbolical; at any rate the supernatural life is not based on them. The super- natural life is the life of prayer. By supernatural means

we do and become things we could not otherwise do or
become; by supernatural means we are linked to God
through Our Lord and his Church. How marvellous
is the supernatural life in the Church, that great
hierarchy and interconnection of souls! Our Lord
always banded people together; a little company and
a head, the Apostles, the family. The parables are full
of all this; always Christ speaks of a little company,
and then their head. He seems always to work that
way: the disciples, then St. Peter, the Church. It is
always a company, a head, never a purely individual
way. Do you sufficiently understand the idea of the
Church—the supernatural life of the Church? the
aggregate of souls in the Church? the two aspects,
the fed, and the feeding side? The Spirit of Our Lord
in the Church, the separate *Person* of the Church,
not simply the piling-on of persons, the addition of
souls, but the separate *Person* of the Church. Both
the communion of souls—the visible body of Christ
and his Spirit on earth—and the invisible Church;
the body and the soul, the Bride of Christ. Yes. And
we are fragments of the Bride.

"I hope you will always follow the mind of the
Church. I like to notice how instinctively you do so
already. People often ask me what religion is for.
What is the use of religion? I do not know how to
answer. I simply cannot say more than this—that
I simply cannot get on without it. I must have it to
moderate me, to water me down, to make me possible.
I am so claimful, so self-occupied, so intense. I want
everything my own way. It is the difficulties and
dangers in people that make them saints. It is almost
impossible to me sometimes to stand people *with* God—

without God it would have been impossible. If I had not had my religion I should have been a blackguard.

"I want to write so plainly and fully in my book about the problem of evil, the power of evil in a world ruled by an omnipotent God the source of all good; we never get rid of this problem. We can only minimise it. There are people who pretend that the earthquake at Tokio was a good thing—to have cancer in the face is somehow splendid, and shows the goodness of God! I hate all that talk. Evil is a mystery, and you don't do away with it by calling it good. People often find strange reasons for disbelieving in God. They say so many things, ask so many questions—about the Inquisition, about Galileo—but they leave out this— the great question—the problem of evil. They strain at a gnat and swallow a camel. I want you so to keep the conception of freedom clear and crisp in your mind. I think you do. There is now a widespread opinion and propaganda which I am sure is shallow and sterilising. According to this view the liability to sin and evil in human beings is inextricably connected with man's freedom, with our being capable of virtue—without the bad, no possibility of evil— the possibility of sin is thus the price of the actuality of virtue and sanctity. This view, if true, might help us in our problem of evil. But is it true? I am sure it is *not*. On this point it is impossible to better St. Augustine's 'To be able not to sin is a great liberty, but to be *unable* to sin is the greatest liberty.' We can at once see this to be true if we think of God.

"How horrible you felt it in that High Churchman's paper when he spoke of potential evil in God! This incapacity to sin is no limit to God's freedom; to be perfectly free means spontaneously to always love and will what is perfectly beautiful, perfectly true, perfectly good. The mere ability to will otherwise is already an imperfection of the will. Hence man can will, can commit evil—*not because he is free,* but because he is *imperfectly* free. The question that remains is why God who doubtless knows well this imperfection, and cannot love it as such, and who cannot but have known the great evils that spring from this imperfection—why did he not make man with a perfect liberty? Man would have been more rather than less good—and all the misery and sin and evil would have been avoided.

"I do not believe in the answer that God wanted a variety of goodness in the world; for here we have an opening of countless degrees of evil. Nor do I believe that God made man thus capable of sin from a prevision that he would fall, and that thus God would raise him, and through the Redemption raise him higher than he would have been without the Fall and the Redemption. For if penitence in man and mercy in God are beautiful things, sin nevertheless is a terrible price to pay for even these. If God could create finite beings incapable of willing evil, a condition of things admirably higher than that of liberty of choice, he would have done so. I believe there is only one way out: to hold as follows:

"Aquinas draws out very fully the doctrine that the Divine Omnipotence must not be taken as the power to effect any imaginable thing, but only the power to effect what is within the nature of things—ultimately according to the nature of God. God

cannot violate his own nature. Now I take it that
whether we see it or not, it is contrary to the nature
of things for a finite being to possess perfect liberty,
to be incapable of violating its true nature (and God
himself, though infinite, cannot create infinite beings).
The real alternative would thus be, not whether
God should create beings with perfect or beings with
imperfect liberty: but only whether the beings whom
alone he could create (beings with imperfect liberty)
would bring more happiness than misery, or more
misery than happiness, into the world; and I take it
that God will have seen that far more happiness than
misery would have been brought into existence by
the creation of beings capable of sin; and he would
have preferred to bring that happiness into being,
even accompanied by this misery.

"I should love you to be penetrated thus by the sense
of this true liberty of God, and by the need for grace,
God's constant prevenience and gift. I want you also
to feel this gift to spring, not from the intensity of
evil in human nature, but from the *weakness* in that
nature. Those who most exalt the power and need of
grace do so usually by most depreciating nature. God
thus gets glorified in direct proportion as man gets
vilified. The more holy I find God, the more wicked
I feel myself to be. This is touching and real, and
almost irresistible to vehement natures, but it is
dangerous and excessive. The inconstancy, variety
and insufficiency of nature—this is the central fact
with us—with its profound need of grace, and its
incapacity to gain grace of itself. I wonder if you
have noticed one more pathetic condition of our little
earthly lot?—that not only even sanctity as it is among

human beings here below is almost always limited in
this or that, or in several directions — but that even
where it is fully great and adequate its delicate
originality is somewhat blunted and blurred before
it can circulate freely amongst the average souls,
which are not comfortable except with something a
little banal and thin. How much I have noticed this!
How much one sees this in the pathetic transformation
that St. Catherine of Genoa's figure has to go through
at the hands of Battista! How much less attractive,
less expansive, less entrancing she becomes than at
the hands of Ettore, and then of the popular devotion!
Popular devotions always need something a little
almost vulgar, somehow. There are parallels of this
even in Biblical writings.

"I wonder if you have seen how much you will be
called on to help people—to help souls. <u>The golden
rule is, to help those we love to escape from us</u>; and
never try to begin to help people, or influence them,
till they ask, but wait for them. Souls are never dittos.
The souls thus to be helped are mostly at quite different
stages from our own, or they have quite a different
attrait. One should wait silent for those who do not
open out to us, who are not intended, perhaps, ever
to be helped by us—except by our prayers (the best
of all helps). We must be tolerant and patient, too,
with those we can, and ought to help. This difference
in souls wakes us up, and makes us more sensitive and
perceptive. Many women are better helped by women
than by men. Yet how few women are sufficiently
trained interiorly to be able to help wisely!

"There are such differences of soul! Some people
are like geometrical patterns. They worship in wide

B

geometrical lines. Others worship a light that fringes off into darkness. Don't try to be like other people, or to make them like you. Puck may want to be a cat, but he can't be a cat. It would be a great pity if he could become a cat. I must wear my own top-hat, and also I must not kick anyone else's top-hat.

"I love Browning's poem *Muléykeh*. It is the story of a man who gives up his mare, his Pearl, because if he kept her she would become less than her best. How beautiful that is, and how touching! I will read it to you. He teaches her himself how to escape from him, though it breaks his own heart.

"Prayer and suffering for others, voluntarily given, is like storing up riches for souls. No one can take the place of others for contrition, but he can, God willing, for satisfaction. Never forget the enormous variety of souls. This will help to develop still more in you the sense of interdependence, the hierarchy of souls —the Church—the Kingdom of Heaven, as conceived and awakened by our Lord.

"It is curious, but it seems to me that some people are quite deficient in the religious sense. I don't understand it at all. They are like people who are without the musical sense. God must allow it, it is somehow his will. Religion to them, is a purely this-world affair. God is a kind of chalk pit. Religion is *not* of this world, it is supernatural, it leavens the world. They can never understand this, and the need for this leaven. The Church works in two levels. She is never the State. She is not the police, nor a sanitary engineer, nor a bricklayer, nor a builder, nor a plumber. Marriage, having children, education, proper clothes, decent behaviour, the plumber—all these are good things, but they are not religion. The essence of religion is the supernatural life; the other world, the otherness of God, different from, but penetrating this our life. That is God's level. The natural level is the State, etc. The Church must never be the State. People put God so far away, in a sort of mist somewhere. I pull their coat-tails. God is *near*. He is no use unless he is near. God's otherness and difference, and his nearness. You *must* get that. God's nearness is straight out of the heart of Jesus. Religion is like a cuckoo in some people's nest. They do not understand man's need. No man is satisfied in a swimming-bath; he knocks his knees and elbows against its sides; he wants the sea. So with man's soul, he hungers and thirsts for the ocean, for God; God infinite and other, different to man, yet working in man. God's givenness. Love, suffering, renunciation, they are God's level; the passion and hunger *for* God comes *from* God, and God answers it with Christ. We are creatures, and we must be creaturely. If you go out and look at the stars, can you be so puffed out, so like a balloon as to think this earth is the only inhabited world of all those millions of stars? Do you think man the only conscious being God has made? Are you so like a balloon? I always tried to teach my children humility. I do not believe we shall ever have the Kingdom of Heaven here, not in this world. The Sermon on the Mount cannot be here. George cannot give the Kaiser his cheek to strike. You cannot give all that you have to the poor. The kingdom cannot be here. That is God's level. Utopias are no use. How boring are Utopias! The hunger and thirst for God in man's soul

can never be answered here; nothing but God himself
is the answer, is any use.

"I always encourage people to practise many non-
religious interests in their lives. It's so important in
helping others, and to keep your own religion full and
mixed. You would find your religion itself grow thin
and poor, sentimental, without this practice. Do not
have too many practices; the soul to grow needs quiet.
I rather hate all these religious conferences and con-
fabulations; I don't believe they do religion much
good. We talk such a lot about toleration nowadays:
take care. In nine cases out of ten toleration means
indifference. What people love and admire most in
people is what they believe: their affirmations, not
their negations. It is not Darwin's negation of religion
we love, but his science of plants: it is not your
father's agnosticism, but his love and joy and his
music that are so precious.

"The central fact of religion is not survival, but
God. I am almost not interested in survival, unless it
means God. Survival must mean God, or it means
nothing at all. There are people who try to prove
God only as a means to immortality; they have got
it all upside down. How secondary is immortality to
God! I always think St. Paul was excessive with his
"Let us eat, drink and be merry," for look at the
Psalmists! They hardly believed in immortality. They
did not think about it. Yet theirs is the deepest expression we know of love of God, of sanctity and
holiness, and of joy. What joy they contain! They
express the joy of the Saints. I do not believe we
should all be sinners without this hope. I do not
believe it.

"To know God here is something—to know him and have union with him here through Our Lord, that would be enough without immortality. Look at St. Catherine of Siena; she saw Heaven here and now in the soul—through its union with God. Heaven is within the soul.

"Hell? Well, God calls you through love—and if the love of God is not enough to make you good, perhaps you had better have fear. It is better to be good somehow, than not to be good at all, if you can't get any further than that.

"People dislike and despise symbols so much nowadays, and yet how necessary they are! They are most inadequate, but that doesn't matter. Once when I was very ill, I dwelt all the time on a picture of the Sacred Heart. It was everything to me, I looked at it and prayed to it all the time, it was the only thing that seemed to make my illness bearable. After some years I saw this picture again: it was odious, vulgar, such a trashy picture! I was ashamed to think what it had been to me—yet it had been everything! You see how the sensible always conveys the spiritual: the invisible in the visible. Christ everywhere makes use of the sensible to convey the spiritual, never the spirit alone. Man is spirit and body; he has arms and legs, he is not spirit alone, he is not even an angel. The spirit is stimulated through the senses—to object to this is foolishness. Christ never left them out: the women who touched him, the clay on the eyes. He always and everywhere makes use of the sensible. Thus the bread and the wine. Man needs the sensible so long as he is man and not spirit alone.

"I want you to hold very clearly, to see as clearly

rel

other
religions

as you can see anything, the truth not that all religions
are true, but that all contain some element of truth,
some fragment from God. But they vary in value—
greater or less—*they are never interchangeable.* God has
never left the world in complete and groping darkness; all religions contain *some* light from God. They
are all from him. It is an awful idea that souls who
cannot have known Our Lord should be debarred
from God. None of the saints believed that. Even now
only one in five people have ever heard of Our
Lord. That's why I don't worry about Baptists and
Unitarians. They can all get into my waistcoat
pocket. The future of Anglicanism seems to me very
dark unless they can revive the sense of adoration. You
can't have religion without adoration. The Reformation was a poor thing, yet some people admire it! It
halved everything, and we do not want the halving of
things, but things at their deepest and fullest. We want
more love, more adoration: more God, more Christ.

"Our bodies are clumsy old fellows, we want too
much of them: we try to express angel faces in worsted,
to play Bach on a penny whistle, Beethoven on a
hurdy-gurdy. The soul lives in two worlds—hence the
tension.

"The essence of sin is to take the jam without the
powder. I want to speak of the abiding consequence
of sin. We seem to be going all wrong here. The
modern non-Catholics are giving this, the abiding
consequences, up altogether. We are so fond of men,
we can't keep God. The most subtle enemy of religion
is humanitarianism. If Christianity is true, there must
be abiding consequences. We can't get rid of it, it's
in all the Gospels. Our Lord speaks of it several times.

His message is an immense warning to us here and
now, a terrific alternative. You must see that. If you
read the Gospels and give that up, I don't know
what you see.

"Purgatory and Hell may be refined, but they must
be there. The majority of souls can't go straight to
Heaven; but God will never turn away from that soul
that turns to him even only at the last. It is *wilful* sin,
the will turning away from God to the very end, that
makes Hell. That soul is *in* Hell that finally rejects
and turns away from God. It must be so. God himself can't alter that, it is the soul's own choice and
abiding-place — the abiding consequences. Sin is a
disharmony. I keep that."

During the last few months of my uncle's life we
had our talks every week as usual, but he was very
tired. He used up all his strength on the book about
God that he wanted so much to finish, he spoke of it
often. He seemed full of a deep peace and content.
I think he felt his work was nearly done. He spoke
very often of Troeltsch, whose death he felt very
keenly. He had hoped to have so much from him, but
"he was much further than I thought from Christianity.
He must have changed a lot of late, more than I knew.
But I like to hope and think that his soul was more
Christian than he knew. I believe he was fundamentally
Christian, and had he lived he would have returned to
it fully and truly. Troeltsch used to laugh at me and
say: 'Baron, you talk and talk. You make out this
and that reason for people doing things, but the real
reason is that people are so stupid.'" He often spoke
of Tyrrell and his restless sceptical mind. "I remember

Troetsch

the very place where Tyrrell said to me, 'We shall go separate ways. You believe in love as the final end, but I believe in love and hate. I believe in the devil, I fight him with hate.' I always felt restless after being with him: one is always restless after being with sceptical minds." He spoke of how difficult it was for young people to understand the need for religion. "They have not enough experience, they need humility; that will come." He spoke of his horror of Pantheism, but how we escaped it through Christ: "A great foot, a pierced foot, prevents that door closing there." "Pantheism as a programme is no use," he said one day. He spoke of young Anglican clergy whom he found too fond of kite-flying. "They seem to have got a kind of Christism now, not God. God is too difficult. Christ is easy. (Is he easy?) They must have everything easy. We hardly need God if we have Christ. How different all this is to Our Lord himself. Did he not come to show us the Father? Well, you can obscure Christ, but you can't shake him. So many people are too clever for religion: we want less brains, more heart. Brains are no use, we want the child. I always try to get the child to come up in people."

He spoke very often of the Catholic Church, of what he owed to her, of what she was, her depth and breadth: "I ask myself which is the greater, depth or breadth? Depth matters most. Rome has that: she is deepest." He spoke of Huvelin: "Sometimes I ask myself—the wisest, widest, deepest men I have known —are not they all Roman Catholics? Yes, they are." He spoke of the sacramental life of the Church; of the great supernatural life and communion of souls, of

God's unique gift to the Church. "Has she not something—something peculiar to her alone, something specific, something unique? There, that's what we want; we cannot do without that. The Roman Catholic Church is like a great ship, first she rolls this way, then she rolls that, till she finds her equilibrium; and then how wise are her judgments! How magnificent her decisions!" Another day he said, "You can't be a Roman for nothing. There is a tension here, a heroism, an other-worldness. If you don't feel it, then it's your fault. There must be some change in you."

I believe there are people who speak of my uncle as a great theologian, but hardly a true member of the Roman Catholic Church. I do not know what to say to these: they seem to me so far from the truth — to know and understand him so little that they have not found him at all. He lived so deeply in his Church's life that I cannot think of him as without her. His whole life and practice were inspired by her teaching and doctrine. He lived within all her boundaries, his mind was knit to, and his soul fed by, her soul. Everything he did was "to be in the mind of the Church." To try and isolate him from what she made is simply not possible, for he would inevitably cease to be all that made him himself. I feel as though I could not speak strongly enough for him here. For to me whom he taught, there was always this note, always this background; the necessity for man of a Church, the basis of all real sanctity; and for the greatest here below, the supernatural life of the Roman Catholic Church, "the deepest of all, spiritually, mystically, supernaturally."

*B

To cut him away from her, and to expect him to live
—as well separate heat from fire, heart-beats from life!

True, he often spoke of Institutional Christianity as
his hair-shirt—his Church his deepest pain. But how
far this is from his *final* word on the subject! Were not
"costingness" and "tension" the two great elements
of growth? Was not pain his greatest teacher? Did not
just such an intense and claimful nature as his require
more than anything the discipline and training, and
the food, of the Roman Catholic Church? He gives
himself a clear answer when discussing this question
(in regard to the Sadhu): "The answer comes clear
and complete. The price is assuredly so great that
only a strong faith can pay it, but the gain is profound.
And I know not whether of anything worth having
for men here below more than this can be said."

The Roman Church was the sap of his spirit, her
life, the life within his own. How we should misunderstand him if we did not get that!

He was constantly affirming to me the need of some
Church appurtenance [1] (just as in prayer he coun-
selled always *some* vocal prayer—Our Father — the
Creed—the Psalms, and one decade of the Rosary
daily; and of course always a daily reading of the
New Testament and the *Imitation* if possible); and for
those biggest souls that he saw and loved, he longed
most of all, that they should eventually find their
home and rest in the Roman Catholic Church,
"that great supernatural home and communion of
souls." He longed for them to accept just "that
relative ordinaryness assuredly costing to human

---

[1] A very favourite word of my uncle's in this connection, meaning
some sort or kind of Church faith and practice.

nature, but uniquely dear to God." Towards the end
he spoke wistfully of these very often, for to him they
seemed not yet sufficiently on their knees.

And yet he trembled at the idea of anyone's changing. (I was not received myself till September 1926.)
He begged one to put off making a decision, to wait
patiently for more light—to avoid all rash judgments
and action.

He was so afraid, lest it was his influence, or one's
love for him making one wish to be where he was,
that made one restless. His reluctance to allow me to
consider, at first, the possibility of my changing from
Anglican to Catholic, was the measure of his sense
of responsibility, his recognition of the difference in
souls, and in their state. "I never want to convert any
soul that is practising in good faith what religion it
possesses," he once said, "I only want to deepen and
strengthen what that soul has already got. But, on
the other hand, if I meet a non-pratiquant Roman
Catholic, I cannot rest for longing till I have brought
it back to some, if not to the full practice of the
Roman Faith."

He told me often of people who had changed under
his influence, and had become poor or even unprac-
tising Catholics—and how he felt himself to blame
in having unsettled them, and given them what they
were not ready for. This was the deepest grief to him:
"When I think of these, and it is quite a long list,
how I wish I had never talked to them!" He saw
too, and valued so greatly, the affirmations of other
churches and religions, that he was anxious one
should not clutch at fuller treasures with unworthy
or unready hands. No doubt as he grew older his

sense of his own dependence made him more and more aware of the vitality, the difference, the *costingness* and reality of his Church's life. For there is another life here—"a heroism" which he loved, a life of which he, more than any, would wish one to be worthy. He feared lest one should step lightly over. Catholicism does not wear all its riches on the outside.

Who can but be touched at this his tender solicitude for each soul's best, his anxiety lest he should be pushing one where one had not yet been called to go? Then he so disliked and distrusted hurry and anticipation—change, excitement and reaction were all his greatest foes; dullness and routine, faithfully accepted, were, he believed, a necessity for the soul's growth. And last, in his most touching confidence, he often told me how he felt sure that God loved and blessed my way and prayer; and that failing any great light to the contrary, I should remain docile and humble, trying to put on one side any impatience or thought of changing, till I felt it clearly a sin to remain where I was.

All this seems to me most wise, a fatherly wisdom. But I do blame myself for not showing him, and saying out more certainly as time passed, that I had found where was my home and necessity. He knew I had never seen the need for any Church till I knew him, nor did I know the possibility of loving any Church till I found his. But this was not enough. I had to show him more—and this I could not do. I was so used to listening and accepting, not explaining. So each time that I grew restless, I tried again to care for what had grown to seem so empty, to follow what he had advised. I loved and practised one way, while joined officially to something to which I felt quite strange, and I tried to remain content in this my double state. I did not see that these alternations were not wholesome, and that there can be difficulties that sterilise, longings unfulfilled that may destroy all enthusiasm and conviction. My soul poised between two centres, and knowing where she should be, began to suffer loss.

But in his knowledge and determination that no emotion or influence should guide one, how right and true that was! And how significant of the truth *au fond* is the fact that when I did change, the call came unadorned by any joy or emotion, only a hard and naked will to follow God was what I found.

Now that he is gone, and one reads his books as a whole, it is impossible not to be deeply impressed by the lovely growth of his mind and soul within that great Communion. He matures and mellows quite clearly beneath our eyes. Towards the end, his whole nature seems to burst into flower, and that gentleness and geniality he loves so much becomes his own. Those "drops of clear religious wine" he speaks of, have purified him of any imperfection and strain; he is full of a touching humility and under-standing, a reaching out to all the other sorts of minds he saw and longed to love. His soul refreshes ours in its clear spring of tenderness and hope. He had, no doubt, to be where truth was fullest, love deepest; no half-way-house could satisfy a soul like his. He needed, too, all that huge tradition, that vast, wide world, that spacious home for every kind of soul and saint.

His passion could find no rest in cold conventionality; and he loved, almost most of all, to share in the homeliness of his great Church. He often asked me to notice in all the pre-Reformation churches and cathedrals, the little touching evidences of a different form of faith. He never failed to say, "in your little *pre-Reformation* church."

Once, years ago, I ignorantly asked him if it were not the same—"just the same thing really" to him, were his friends Catholics or of any other sort of faith?

I do not forget his answer, I do not forget his face. The stupidity of my question quite upset him—and after a pause, he said, looking rather distressed, "The same thing—how can it be the same thing? My little old thing, you do not understand. I love many Anglicans, High Church, Broad—Unitarians, Presbyterians—yes—yes—all—many. But it is not *the same thing* to me—it can never be the *same thing*": then, in his deepest, most vibrant tones, "I am a child of the Confessional—I am a son of the great Roman Church."

A few days before he died he said, "I wait for the breath of God, for God's breath. Perhaps he will call me to-day—to-night. Don't let us be niggardly towards God. He is never a niggard towards us.—Let us try to be generous and accept.—My illness is so little! I have no pain—my brain is clear—why should I not accept this generously? I would like to finish my book—but if not, I shall live it out in the Beyond. —I love the angels, they stand for something we cannot otherwise express. . . .

"Plant yourself on foundations that are secure— God—Christ—Suffering—the Cross. They are secure. How I love the Sacraments! I am as certain of the Real Presence of Christ in the Eucharist as of anything there is. Our great hope is in Christianity—our only hope. Christ re-creates. Christianity has taught us to care. Caring is the greatest thing—caring matters most. My faith is not enough—it comes and goes. I have it about some things and not about others. So we make up and supplement each other. We give and others give to us. Keep your life a life of prayer, dearie.—Keep it like that: it's the only thing, and remember, no joy without suffering—no patience without trial—no humility without humiliation—no life without death."

I was ill with influenza when my uncle died, and I saw him for the last time four days before his death. He was very tired and weak, and everything was a great effort. But he spoke of nearly everyone—he seemed to be recalling them one by one. He spoke, too, of the Resurrection.

When I look back on all these talks, the letters and this companionship, I know them to be the greatest privilege and joy I shall ever receive. If I have learnt anything, it is from him that I learned—and with him there went a great dignity out of life. But I have never felt sad or separated from him. How should I? What he taught me has carried me on.

"Our Lord is full of a great tenderness—tenderness and austerity. There is no tenderness without austerity —no love or greatness almost, without it. Our Lord saw that suffering was knit into human nature, but he does not become morbid over it. He sees it is not the end. He sees the coming of joy, the suffering ending in the crown—the coming of joy through and because of this suffering."

I was already thirty-eight when first my uncle

began to teach me. I had known him as a child, but I was afraid of him then. I was afraid first of his deafness and of his ear-trumpet; and next I was afraid of his strangeness. When I saw him at my grandmother's I always hoped I would not have to sit next to him at luncheon. I liked to watch him, but I dreaded to attract his attention. He seemed to me something so different and unordinary, something rather wild, a being belonging to another world. When, years later, he first began to talk to me, he told me how he had never forgotten the strange little girl who used to sit and stare at him—and how he had said to my aunt, "I feel so sorry for that poor little thing; she will never fit into this world, she comes from another star." These words of his are so characteristic, and they comfort one too. For they show that though we cannot be the same in degree, we can share in kind with what we love most.

Here, at the end, with so much left out and forgotten, I must stop. The least and the last of his many friends, I can speak less than any of those deepest things that he spent his life in pursuing. I can say so little of his passionate search for truth: in philosophy, theology, religion; in life and in love: he sought, apprehended, suffered and pursued, with a faith that ended only with his death. How much he found! I am confused to tell of even the beginnings. He saw "certain dim assurances"; he worshipped "a light that fringes off into darkness"; he found the reality of God, and the entire *givenness* of all our spiritual life, love, and prayer. To these things his soul vibrated; they made a commotion within his whole being that one would be blind not to see.

Through suffering he discovered joy, and to his "final note of joy" he added love.

"Christianity taught us to care. Caring is the greatest thing, caring matters most." These seem to me his last most final words, uttered in a voice so small and still and far away, it seemed hardly his own.

Love and joy are the way; for joy without love could have no being: love and joy together, springing up united from suffering here below, rise in adoration to find God.

GWENDOLEN GREENE.

In Festo B.M.V. de Monte Carmelo, 1928.

LETTERS

My very dear Gwen,   25 April, 1918.

Your Aunt Mary showed me your plucky letter
received by her yesterday morning. I was in church
at Holy Communion this morning, and I then prayed
and thought very specially of my very dear Niece—
that every deep, rich growth, happiness and faith-
fulness may attend and fulfil her life and work and
sufferings and various joys. Four points occurred to
me—I will put them down here for you, since now,
lying up, you may care to let them simmer in your
heart, and to get them to bloom into action or habit.
This, however in proportion, *pray*—as any of it really
comes home to, really fits your own sight or search—
such things ought always to feel, at first, as just a
size or two too big for us—as what gently stimulates
us to a further growth and expansion; but they should
always be quietly ignored, if, and in so far as they
come before our quiet look at them as conundrums
simply imposed on us from without.

(1) I am, then, really grateful (given you are run
down and require a rest) that you are, plainly, much
worn and tired—for only so would you give up for a
bit, and get looked after properly, and thoroughly
rested back into full power, and it will be delightful
if, without straining, you can now and then quietly
browse through that charming Boissier or Horace

3

and Virgil—and perhaps this or that other of the
books on Roman things.

(2) . . .

(3) I continue much struck, my very dear Gwen,
with your (very rare) youthfulness and keen ardour
of mind. Your continuous openness to the impressions
(fresh as ever) brought you by all things beautiful
and true and good. Do you *realise* how rare this gift
is? That it *is* a gift, one of the most precious of the
gifts—of God? That it is a form and kind of deep
faith—a true prayer? I ask all this that you may mix
with these admirations, more and more, little exclama-
tions of gratitude, of union with, of adoration of God,
present in all this truth, beauty, and goodness. You
could gradually develop this into spontaneous habit.

(4) For years I have loved and prayed this prayer,
Dearie. If it makes sense to you, you too might begin
your day with it. "Receive, O Lord, my entire liberty
—my understanding, my memory, my will. From
Thee I have received all things—to Thee do I return
all things. Give me but Thy Grace and Thy Love.
I ask not anything else of Thee." [1] . . .

Loving old Uncle,
Freddy H.

My very dear Gwen,   30 September, 1918.

This is a letter all about your most dear father
only, of course. But, being thus, you may not feel it
inopportune—you may even like to have it for rumina-
tion since, though you must be longing to help, there
cannot be much, at least of an external, practical kind,
that you *can* do for him, just now.

[1] St. Ignatius.

Well, then, first I want to say how *deeply* I care, how *deeply* I mind. I have known your father for nearly half a century; during all that time I have been getting to know fresh people, and have been getting to know those I knew already far more widely and deeply, I believe. And yet I have never, before those years or during them, known a man so utterly generous, so essentially lovable, as your father. Of course I know well, besides, that he is a real genius—a genius of a large, rare kind—a genius in music. But though I admire this, and I thank God for it—this, in itself, is nothing lovable. What I love so in him is his radiant lovingness—that rich spending, without thought of its being anything other than simply natural, utterly delightful, of a loving heart, upon whomsoever he may meet who at all appeals to it. And the appeal is felt to come, not from the apparent cleverness, or riches, or charm, but simply from the fellow-creature's need and cry for help and sympathy. What an untold *world* of kindness, of paternal help and warmth, he must have given away throughout all these years at the college.

It is, then, a deep, deep grief, Gwen, to have to fear, from your letter, that we are probably about to lose him, in and during this our little earthly life. Then, next, I want to confess to you a prick and a pang of conscience which has been with me concerning him ever since we travelled down to Wilton together for your Uncle Mingo's funeral. I suppose I was overwrought or something else odd and abnormal, but, anyhow, I told him in starting on the journey, that I did not want to converse—especially not about music. Alas, alas: how rude, how impertinent, how entirely contrary to my own self when reasonable at all! I have longed to find the opportunity to beg his kind pardon for this—but have never seemed to find it without making a fuss somehow. So, my dear child, you who have inherited so much of his glorious generosity—tell God for me, by your father's side, how deeply I love him, how vexed I continue with myself about that silly act of mine.

And lastly, my Niece, let me say one little word about a much deeper matter. Your father, Dear, like your also fine-charactered uncle, George—grew up, and lived to middle life, during a religiously sceptical time—they could hardly escape that all-pervading atmosphere—in any case they did not escape it. I love to feel that, even in those times, your father believed more than he thought he did; and again that, since then, he has quite possibly silently come to considerably more belief, even in his own consciousness concerning his convictions. I should dearly like, if he is still sufficiently, for short whiles, himself, that you should ask him quite simply to affirm his faith, his love in God—or, better still, some little aspiration directly to God Himself.

With entire resignation into His hands,

F. v. H.

13 VICARAGE GATE, KENSINGTON, W.

My very dear Gwen,   9 October, 1918.

Oh, we are sad at his having gone—the generous, simple, loving soul—the genius with a heart of a boy and yet with all a father's tenderness for quite

a world of souls. You evidently expected this ending—
you—Gwen, did. But your mother, poor thing, may
have gone on hoping to the end, in which case the
shock of his going will, we fear, be all the greater.
How devotedly he loved on, from the first and un-
ceasingly to the end! There, too—so fine a man; for
such things are not mere accidents—they show a
man's—his—nobility of nature.

I trust and fancy that he did not suffer much, even
at the end. If so, that will have been a great relief
to you all, for him so extra-alive, so sensitive a con-
stitution and nature. Much as I feel for you, very
dear Niece—for you so like him in many ways—and
for Dolly, who also loved him so much and who was
so much loved by him: I yet feel most sorry somehow
—next, of course, to your mother—for that world of
his at the College of Music. The loss to hundreds of
men and women, young and now middle-aged, who
were there, or are still there—must be literally
irreplaceable—irreparable, because your father was
not simply a man who knew his business—nor even a
man of real or great talent; no, but because he was a
man of deep genius, and who, as such, could divine
when any scraps of genius were lurking in others, and
irreparable, even more, because his combination of
such genius with his, in any walk of life, most rare
steadiness and volume of selfless interest and affection
—of truly parental character—is doubtless specially
rare amongst musicians. Certainly Beethoven was not
like that, nor Wagner. . . .

Forgive absence of mourning paper.

My very dear Gwen,   11 December, 1918.

No letter you will ever write to me shall, please God, ever remain unanswered—shall remain without a reply as careful and complete as I can manage to make it. But you may have to wait a bit, my Niece. I never could write with ease—not on such subjects, where we should never write, speak, or think except with *voce di petto*, never with *voce di testa*. And now I am still weak, and empty of brain, hence a further delay.

Let me make *three or four points* of your letter; and try to explain these as well as I now can manage.

1. The gradual preparation for, and God's revelations preceding, His fullest self-revelation in Christianity.

I am very glad you apprehend and appreciate this great fact—a fact, however, which you will have to learn to apply, not only to *the succession of history*, but also to the *simultaneous present*. What I mean is that, not only was Judaism especially, yet also, in lesser and other degrees, Hellenism, Hinduism, etc., an historically previous preparation by God Himself for the fuller and fullest self-revelation; but this *holds still* of those imperfect, mixed forms and degrees of light, in so far as they still continue distinct in the world. The synagogue here in Bayswater is still now, on 11 December, 1918, a fragmentary but very real revelation of God and, however unconsciously, a very real pedagogue to Christ. The little mosque at Woking is still, for some souls, a yet more fragmentary but still real revelation of God and teacher of truths more completely taught by Christianity. All this, however, only in so far as the souls thus helped have no interior incitement to move on and up into a fuller, truer religion. And nothing of all this means that these various religions are equally true (or false), and that it does not matter to which you belong (provided only you are in good faith). No: in these deepest and most delicate of all matters, even a little more light, more power, more reality—even what "looks" a "little"—means, and is very, profoundly much. It all only means, that nowhere does God leave Himself without *some* witness, and without *some* capacity on the part of the soul (*always more or less costingly*) to respond to, and to execute this His witness. And, again, that everywhere the means and the process are from fidelity to the light already possessed (yet often difficult to see owing to the agitations and cowardice of the soul), to further light, which again, in its turn, demands a delicate, difficult fidelity and fresh sacrifices. Yet with each such fidelity and sacrifice, the peace, the power, the joy, the humble fruitfulness of the soul grow. Always it is a search for expansion and happiness, found in acts gently costly and increasingly exacting.

2. Only the best attractive to you; and any, every church, very middling, hence dull, repulsive. Thus you do not go to country church services, etc.

The touching, entrancing beauty of Christianity, my Niece, depends upon a subtle something which all this fastidiousness ignores. Its greatness, its special genius, consists, as much as in anything else, in that it is without this fastidiousness. A soul that is, I do not

say tempted, but dominated, by such fastidiousness,
is as yet only hovering round the precincts of Christianity, but it has not entered its sanctuary, where
heroism is always homely, where the best always acts
as a stimulus towards helping towards being (in a
true sense) but one of the semi-articulate, bovine,
childish, repulsively second-third-fourth-rate crowd.
So it was with Jesus Himself; so it was with Francis,
the Poverello; so it is with every soul that has fully
realised the genius of the Christian paradox. When
I told you of my choking emotion in reading, in
St. John's Gospel, that scene of Jesus, the Light of
the World (that He is this, is an historic fact), as the
menial servant at the feet of those foolish little fisher-
men and tax-gatherers, what do you think moved me
but just that huge, life-and-love-bringing paradox,
here in its fullest activity? The heathen philosophies,
one and all, failed to get beyond your fastidiousness:
only Christianity got beyond it; only Christianity.
But I mean a deeply, *costingly* realised, Christianity—
got beyond it: Gwen will, some day, get beyond it.
It is, really, a very hideous thing; the full, truly free,
beauty of Christ alone completely liberates us from
this miserable bondage.

"Well, perhaps yes," you will say, "but what am
I, here and now, to do?" Do, as to church-going,
nothing but what you already do. Only be very conscientious and regular in going to your Holy Communions, whether in country or town, and in going
to church every Sunday when you are in town. But
as to your thinking and speaking, pray, and ruminate,
Niece, over what I have been saying; look out in your
readings for what confirms it; grow shy of any defence

of fastidiousness; pray to God gradually to cure you of it, if and when you come fairly to see it to be a poor, a very poor, thing. You rightly dislike Pater's "affectation." What I call "preciousness." Well, in face of the dread facts of human nature, and of the rich teaching of history, that church-fastidiousness is a sort of Paterism.

3. What is the precise meaning of Thekla's insistence upon religion as primarily an is-ness, not an ought-ness?

A good question. Well, you see, Niece, when the Renaissance and the Protestant Reformation, and later the French Revolution came, they, in part, only articulated, but also they, in part, each differently, yet all greatly, fed and excited a reaction which had permeated the educated average man of Western Europe ever since, say, A.D. 1300. It was a reaction away from the (by then too exclusive) occupation with the object—with *things*, taken as though apprehended by us without our minds, and especially with *supernatural things*, taken as so different in kind from our natural endowments, as to require a sheer imposing from without—a simple plastering on to the human soul and mind. These doctrines, against which there came the reaction, are *not* the doctrines really held by the Middle Ages at their best—say, from A.D. 1100 to A.D. 1300, but they were the doctrines of the later, moribund Middle Ages, and they were doctrines by which those Renaissance, Reformation and Revolution doctrinaires were really profoundly infected—as is always the case with men who do not patiently study the past (also the more recent past) and who, instead of discriminating, condemn what is

before them *as it stands*—who do not untie knots, but
who cut them. Again, Dear, do you note? Life taken
cheaply—"cheaply," I mean, because practised and
sought outside of, and not within, and by working
through, its entanglements! Well, now, these three
(and other) specifically "modern" movements have
been very largely dominated by a most ruinous,
excessive, or even exclusive insistence upon the *subject*
—your own (or at least humanity's) apprehending
powers, feelings, etc. *These subjective* powers get, here,
more or less taken as alone certain, as always the first
facts in the order of our life and consciousness. Thus,
a baby will be taken first to feel, know himself—or
rather, his own feeling and knowing, and then gradually
to discover an outside world—his mother's breast, his
nurse's hand, his cradle soft or hard, etc.—all this
being really less certain (in itself, or at least for his
mind) than is his thus feeling, knowing himself. You
entirely follow?

Well, then, even more as to God—the supersensible,
the Infinite—He is pushed still farther back amongst
the late-acquired, the more or less doubtful "ideas,"
"notions," "perhapses."—The regulative notions for
our conduct, the useful, more or less, working answer
to our real difficulties amongst our real facts.—An
hypothesis, "it is useful to live *as though* there were a
God"? Kant's celebrated "als ob"? Conduct here
alone is quite certain; but then, too, conduct alone
entirely matters. Religion is here always directly
dependent upon, it is but the (really derivative,
though seemingly superior) sanction of morality. How
different is real life, and the spontaneous attitude of
all unsophisticated religion! In real life (all good

psychologists and all careful theorists of knowledge are coming to see it) there is from *the first* direct contact with, direct knowledge of realities other than ourselves. Light and air, plants, animals, fellow-humans, the mother, the nurse: these are known together with ourselves—we never know ourselves except with and through those realities, and with and through our knowledge of them. Indeed, it is them we know best first; we know ourselves, at all adequately, only last of all. This knowledge of other realities less than human or simply human is never a knowledge through and through—it never simply equals the reality known. But it is a real knowledge of these realities, as far as it goes; realities which reveal their natures in their various self-manifestations. I know Puck as truly as Puck knows me; my knowledge does not merely extend to appearances of him—appearances hiding, and probably travestying, his mysterious, simply unknowable essence.

We thus certainly know other realities besides our human reality (whether individual or even collective). And mark you, if this very real knowledge of realities not ourselves, always lags behind those realities as they are in themselves: *this knowledge, nevertheless, is (or can be) fuller than any complete and clear analysis of it can ever be.* Thus reality comes first; then knowledge of it; then science of this knowledge.

What about God? Well, we must first of all become clear to ourselves that, *as with every degree and kind of reality*, we always apprehend Him only in, and with, and on occasion of, yet also in contrast to, other realities. Again, that this apprehension and sense of God is (where not worked up and developed by the

great historical, institutional religions) very vague and
general, if taken as something statable in theoretical
terms. (Here again, then, is the difference between
knowledge and science!) Nevertheless, thus defined,
the religious sense exercises a *prodigious* influence. It
is the religious sense, even at this stage, where it seems
no more (on strict analysis) than a deep, delicate,
obstinate sense of otherness, of eternity, of prevenience,
of more than merely human beauty, truth, and
goodness, which really keeps our poor little human
world a-going. No great artist, no great philosopher
or scientist, no great ethical striver will ever fully,
consciously, and deliberately admit that what he
strives to paint, to sculpt, to compose, or to discover
or to understand, or to live and to be, is just human
so-and-so-ness, very possibly without any further
significance or truth about it whatsoever.

We have to be truthful, conscientious: why? Because
these are the dispositions for putting us into fuller
touch with realities of all sorts, especially with the
reality of God. Dispositions are the means to acquiring
reality—towards knowing, loving, willing realities
greater than ourselves—in which energisings we grow
in our own smaller reality.

When, then, Thekla says "religion has primarily
to do with is-ness not ought-ness," she means that
religion is essentially evidential; that it intimates,
first of all, that a superhuman world, a superhuman
reality *is*, exists. The first and central act of religion
is *adoration*, sense of God. His otherness though nearness, His distinctness from all finite beings, though not
separateness—aloofness—from them. If I cannot completely know even a daisy, still less can I ever completely

know God. One of the councils of the Church launched the anathema against all who should declare that God is comprehensible. Yet God too, God in some real sense especially, we can most really know, since as does even the rose how much more He? Since <u>He deigns to reveal Himself to us. He does so in a two-fold manner—vaguely, but most powerfully—in the various laws and exigencies of life, and of our knowledge of it; and clearly, concretely, in and by the historic manifestations in and through the great geniuses and revealers of religion</u>—the prophets, and especially Jesus Christ. These latter manifestations get thoroughly learnt only in and through the various historical religious bodies. It is through men trained through and through in these schools of religion that all the more solid and sane insights and habits, even of the vague religion, get given most of the point and steadiness which, as a matter of fact, they possess.

4. There is not a line of all the above which has not to be learnt in careful detail, in lowly practice, in humble daily fight with self—in docility and docility on and on. We will gradually, ruminatingly, get the whole unrolled before us. The all-important point is, I think, at each step to feel how rich, how inexhaustible, how live it all really is! That is why I am trying to get such words as "Rome," "Athens," etc. to mean a great rich world to you.

Gradually I shall give you more directly religious books to ponder; yet, to the end, these should be made to penetrate and purify a whole mass of not directly religious material and life. <u>God is the God of Nature as of Grace</u>, He provides the meal and the

c

yeast. Let us act in accordance with this, His own action.

Affec. Uncle,

F. v. H.

EXTRACT FROM LETTER DATED 23 JANUARY, 1919

I am sorry but not a bit surprised that you have been finding *Varro* a bit dull—even though he be presented by Boissier, who assuredly is in no wise the cause of this dullness. But I felt, Niece mine, that I must thus risk, now and then, say once in ten times, to give you something that will a bit bore you. No: I felt something more and other than that. You see, Niece, one reason why there are, as I think, so few at all large, strong minds and characters about nowadays, even in spite of the war, etc., is that education, training of all sorts, religion even, have been and are so largely pursued systematically as so much beguilement, so much sheer kindergarten. The dullness, the monotony, the hardness, the sheer trust as to worthwhileness, the self-discipline, the asceticism: all this is to count as old fogey-ness: and the result is? Well, wayward childishness. At eighteen I made up my mind to go into moral and religious training. The great soul and mind who took me in hand—a noble Dominican—warned me—You want to grow in virtue, to serve God, to love Christ? Well, you will grow in and attain to these things if you will make them a slow and sure, an utterly real, a mountain step-plod and ascent, willing to have to camp for weeks or months in spiritual desolation, darkness and emptiness at different stages in your march and growth. All demand for constant light, for ever the best—the

best to your own feeling, all the attempt at eliminating
or minimising the cross and trial, is so much soft folly
and puerile trifling. And what Father Raymond
Hecking taught me as to spirituality is, of course,
also true in its way of all study worthy the name.
But *L'Opposition* and the big and little Juvenal will,
I think, not bore you at all—all the less as coming
from what did.

The Letters of the Younger Pliny.

These are truly silver literature, and without the
genius that stamps the work of his close friend Tacitus
as world-literature of the first rank. Yet how charming
they are ! How much I hope you will browse on these
utterly leisurely letters and learn much—very much,
not only about the Roman character already so
pathetically but half, but a tenth part, aware of the
great light and life and love of Christianity—but about
the human heart, the human soul—what I aim at
after all as the end crown of your reading.

How wonderful in this way is his letter to Trajan
about the Christians—how delightful all his relations
with that emperor, one of my dearest figures! How
impressive his account of the fall of Pompeii, and so
on and on!

You will read it all please, at least twice, with the
Life, etc., as well. I deeply regret that I have not been
able to find a translation of P.'s *Panegyric of Trajan*—
that touching piece. I will continue to try for perhaps
a French rendering.

Your very affec. old Uncle,

F. v. Hügel.

Health, stationary still.

13 VICARAGE GATE, KENSINGTON

My dear Gwen,   31 January, 1919.

Thank you much for your good letter. I sent you this morning your new pagan—Rome, packet—five volumes, all of which are presents, so there is nothing even to come back this time.

Please attend to the following points:

1. The Virgil is, you will see, simply the second, last volume of the prose translation, and which you already possess. . . .

Altogether I should love it, if you ended by reading again and again all the first eight books of the Æneid; certainly the culmination of Virgil's lovely genius; the Sixth Book in particular has a mild splendour unsurpassed in all human literature. On the other hand I would counsel you against ever reading the minor poems—all given in this second volume. They are all very slight affairs, certainly *not* by Virgil, and quite unworthy of him. We have such grand other things to get through, and so many of them — we will not waste our precious time over insignificant trifles.

2. As to the Tacitus, I should wish you to do him first amongst the books of the packet. And pray study *the minor* writings first. I want you to read, very slowly, ruminatingly, comparing part with part, etc., the *Dialogue of the Orators*—it will teach you lots as to the strength and the weakness of this "silver age" Roman education. Next, the *Agricola*—this, like the *Dialogue*, at least twice, looking up all the British places on the map, and watching not only for interesting political and military details, but also for touches of the char-

acter of Agricola and of Tacitus himself—both such
fine examples of the best Romans, who passed through
the Terror under Domitian, on to the "Indian
summer" of Rome's imperial times under Trajan,
Hadrian, Antoninus Pius, and Marcus Aurelius. At
least, this is true of Tacitus and of him only up to
and into the reign of Trajan—upon the whole Rome's
happiest time during the four centuries of the Empire.
The *Germania* I always feel to be much less rich in
content than its two predecessors, still it *is* interesting,
especially again nowadays. Perhaps one careful reading
will be enough for this.

Only after all three minor writings and (of course)
the translator's Introduction to them, will you tackle
Tacitus's *Histories*. Please first carefully study the Introduction, and use throughout very capitally clear maps
in the covers—the maps in one volume whilst studying
the other volume. Thus you can have the maps open
before you all the time. But please note, not to force
yourself to get any very clear, very detailed conceptions as to the successive steps of the campaigns, etc.;
concentrate, on the contrary, on T.'s superb portraits
of characters, and his always noble, majestic ideals
and indignation. Even the vilest facts will not hurt
you, when thus lit up and all their grossness con-
sumed by this glorious soul's magnificent ardour. You
could carefully mark these passages, and could then
read these very carefully three times. Note, too, very
specially, the entire book concerning the Jewish War,
and Tacitus's pathetic misconception of the Jewish
religion, and of Christianity. This book is certainly
to be read twice.—I believe now, after all, the *Annals*,
which were my former favourites, are less perfect than

these *Histories*. How I wish you knew Latin, to be able to read Tacitus's magnificence in his own language! Yet some of his splendour will reach you even in the English.

I am gradually getting your next packet ready— it is planned as the last pagan Roman packet, and will be, I hope and think, most valuable as a part of your course—it will lift up the Christian authors in all sorts of ways.—But, before then, you will carefully read, when Varro is mastered, also that charming *L'Opposition sous les Césars* (Boissier) with those grand Juvenal-Johnson poems.

What a fresh, further surprise and blotting-out of old landmarks is this General Election! I must not pretend to be other than very glad and relieved that the Coalition has been strongly backed and settled in. But three things in increasing order distress me. I feel that we must somehow have Mr. Asquith in the House; the returns by majorities of 8000 and 2000 respectively of such unprincipled but most mischievous wind-bags as Bottomley and Billings shows sadly clearly the weak side of all democratic excitement; and the sweeping victory of Sinn Fein, and with actually that woman lunatic returned in Dublin, shows still more clearly how little men are really dominated only, or even chiefly, by reason; in very large numbers, not by reason, but by passion—a very different thing!

My dear Gwen, I trust that even already you feel what a support against such windy impulsions, against such wild rootlessness, is the habitual living in a world steeped in history, in knowledge of the human heart —your own, first and foremost, and, above all, in a sense of the presence, the power, the prevenience of God, the healing Divine Dwarfer of our poor little man-centred, indeed even self-centred, schemes. God bless you, then, Niece, at and for the New Year, very specially.

Loving Uncle,
Freddy.

Best wishes also to your Harry, and to Olivia, Richard, and David.

13 VICARAGE GATE, KENSINGTON, W.8

My dearest Niece,   10 March, 1919.

You asked me in your last letter to write again soon; and hence I do so, as to two points in your reading, and in your mental habits generally, which I am confident you will find of great advantage. I have myself practised and tested these habits now for some thirty years with very great fruit.

1. Whenever you study a book which is yours, cultivate the habit of pencil-marking it, in a small hand, with a sharp-pointed pencil, as follows: (i.) Use the *inner* margins of the pages for references as to words, phrases—form generally; and the *outer* margins for references as to persons, places, doctrines, facts and things generally. You slightly underline, with a short horizontal line, the word or words that strike you. If they strike you as to *form* you put, on the inner margin, at the corresponding height of the page, the number of the other page or pages on which (before or after this page) the same word or phrase occurs. If the passage strikes you as to its *content*, you put on the outer margin

the numbers of the other pages on which these contents occur again. In fact, you form your book into a sort of Reference Bible. Thus, for instance, in your Pliny the Younger, any special garden arrangements, or special points of his Bithynian administration, or particulars as to the heathen cults or as to Christianity, would be thus marked and marginally annotated with the numbers of the pages on which further details as to these several things can be found. Note, please, that for translations one only marks and refers for things; and that only in originals (hence, with you, only in books originally written in English or French) will one have underlinings for *both* things and expressions. Hence, Cæsar, Tacitus, Pliny, etc., would only have outer margin references. But Boissier, etc., would have references also on the inner margins, just as Shakespeare, etc., would have them.

Then, on the fly-leaves at the *beginning* of the books that belong to you, I would, in short words of headings, put down the points as to things that you specially love, or have most learnt from, in the book, with the numbers of the pages in which these several things are discussed; and on the fly-leaves at the end of the same book, I would similarly put down the things I have not liked, that I object to.

You would find that this twice double system of annotation makes the reading sink ever so much more lastingly into you, and that only thus can you readily find again all the things that have specially helped you.

2. Strive hard (especially now you will be coming to the directly Christian books) to attain one of two possible frames of mind. It will be only if you can manage to make the right frame of mind into your

second nature, that you will deserve to grow in insight, love and fruitfulness, my little Gwen.

(i.) You could try and force yourself to see, or to pretend to yourself that you see, principles or convictions advanced by men holy or revered. Do nothing of the kind: you would only lose your sincerity, you would but prepare for yourself a dangerous reaction, and you would not really thus come to see a single step farther than you already see.

(ii.) Or (and this is, I think, for all of us the more immediate fault) you could concentrate on your own, present, explicit not-seeing of a thing, so as to decide that it does not exist, or (at least) that it never can or will be seen as true by yourself. This is doubtless the chief reason why so few minds grow in their outlook after, say, eighteen or twenty-one: they are so busy, pompously affirming to themselves and others that they don't and can't see this or that—that this is not, and that can't be—as to harden down, for good and all, into their narrow, stuffy little world. They thus confuse two very distinct things—sincerity concerning the insight they have got, with striving to acquire further, deeper, truer insight. It is, of course, profoundly true that we get to see more and better by being very faithful and very operative with regard to the light we have. But, then, this fidelity and operativeness should be very humble, very certain that there exist oceans of reality—of things and laws beautiful, true, good and holy, beyond this our present insight and operation. I so love to watch cows as they browse at the borders, up against the hedges of fields. They move along, with their great tongues drawing in just only what they can assimilate; yes—but without stopping

to snort defiantly against what does not thus suit them.
It is as though those creatures had the good sense to
realise that those plants which do not suit them—
that these will be gladly used up by sheep, goats or
horses; indeed, that some of these plants may suit
them—the cows—themselves later on. So ought we
to do: not sniff and snort at what we do not understand here and now; not proclaim, as though it were
a fact interesting to anyone but ourselves, that we do
not, here and now, understand this or that thing; but
we should just merely, quite quietly, let such things
stand over, as possibly very true, though to us they
look very foolish—as indeed, possibly, things that we
ourselves will come to penetrate as true and rich indeed.
In a word, we can and should be sure of all that is
positive and fruitful for us in our outlook; sure, also,
that whatever really contradicts *that* is false. But as to
possible further truths and facts, we will leave ourselves
peacefully docile and open.

13 VICARAGE GATE, KENSINGTON, W.8

My most dear Gwen,   7 April, 1919.

Your letter has set me thinking—re-thinking your
mind and soul, and how best quietly to feed and help
them. I wanted to write an answer on Saturday, and
then to-day. But my last four or five nights have been,
upon the whole, so bad that I dare not yet write
directly about your very important and delicate points,
since, when I am in such "en-compôte" condition,
such letter-writing means further bad nights. I will
write as soon as I can. This is only a scribble, lest my

silence were to end in making you fear indifference or offendedness on my part—neither of which would be at all the case.

I wonder whether you realise a deep, great fact? That souls—all human souls—are deeply interconnected? That, I mean, we can not only pray for each other, but *suffer* for each other? That these long, trying wakings, that I was able to offer them to God and to Christ for my Gwen-child—that He might ever strengthen, sweeten, steady her in her true, simple, humble love and dependence upon Him? Nothing is more real than this interconnection—this gracious power put by God Himself into the very heart of our infirmities. And, my little Gwen, it is the Church (which, improperly understood, "dumbs" my little old, bewildered Child)—it is the Church which, at its best and deepest, is just that—that interdependence of all the broken and the meek, all the self-oblivion, all the reaching-out to God and souls which certainly "pins down" neither my child nor this her old groping father—which, if it "pins down" at all, does so, really only—even taken simply intellectually—as the skeleton "pins down" the flesh. What a hideous thing the skeleton, taken separately, is, isn't it? Yet even Cleopatra, when in the splendour of her youth, she had such a very useful, very necessary, quite unavoidable skeleton inside her, had she not?

But this will be better explained another time. Meanwhile we will both breast the waves, whether sweet or bitter, looking not at them, but through them on and up to God, our Peace.

13 VICARAGE GATE, KENSINGTON, W.8

My very dear Gwen,   5 May, 1919.

Here I am writing to you, in your new temporary home, looking out of your window, I expect, upon how much of past history recorded in gloriously beautiful monuments, poems in stone! And I am doing as my first act (after an urgent business card), on this my birthday, this my scribble to you. I am, dear, dear, sixty-seven years old to-day! Thus, dear Child—you might almost be my granddaughter—do I strive to attain to the joy of Princess Colombe, in Browning's touching play. You remember how she, Colombe, had, up to her coming of age, always received countless sumptuous presents—and she had found only pleasure, and less and less pleasure, in such receiving. So then she settled she would receive no gifts at all on this, the first day on which she could order her own life in her own way; but she would herself give and give and give. She felt *that* would bring—not pleasure, but joy, but beatitude. And so it did—Colombe finishes her day radiantly happy. So, then, sit on a footstool here, by me, Daughter; and I will try and give you —not exterior things, but interior things—things that cost one a lot to get, a lot to keep. They are things, indeed, that also cost one a good deal to give—and I can clearly tell you why, my Gwen. Look you, Dear: there is simply *nothing* that one soul can transfer to another soul—even at these souls' best—with the particular connotations, the particular experiences of heart and heart, of blood and breeding, of sex and age, etc., yet it is these particularities which incarnate the convictions of any one soul for that one soul. Any

one soul can be fully impressive for another soul
only if that first soul comes out, to the second soul,
with its convictions clothed and coloured by those
its particularities. And yet the second soul, even if
thus impressed—even if it thus wakes up to great
spiritual facts and laws,—this second soul will at once,
quite spontaneously, most rightly, clothe and colour
these its new convictions with its own special qualities
and habits and experiences of thought, feeling, imagination, memory, volition; and so—most really—to try
and help on the life of another soul means, Dear, a
specially large double death to self on the part of the
life-bringing soul. For it means death to self before
and in the communication—the life-bringing soul
must already, then, discriminate within itself between
the essence of what it has to say and the accidents,
the particularities, which clothe the utterance of this
essence; and it must peacefully anticipate the acceptance *at most* of that essence, and not of these accidents.
And then, after the communication, this soul must
be ready actually to back the other soul in the non-
acceptance even of the essence of the message, if there
is evidence that the other soul is not really helped,
but is hindered, at least for the time being, by this
essence now offered to it. And, as already said, at
best, *only that essence* can and should be taken over by
this other soul, and the light-bearing soul, even then,
must at once be busy helping the less experienced
soul to clothe the newly won essence in clothing from
the wardrobe of this other soul.

My Gwen, you see, this now, as follows, is the point
which, with the sendings of books which I begin to-
day, I hope you may end by seeing clearly, steadily,

in your quite individual manner and degree. You
see, *I* see, how deep, and dear, how precious, is your
faith in God and in Christ. I thank God for them, and
if to the end you cannot acquire, without really
distracting or weakening that faith, a strong and
serene insight and instinct concerning the great
occasions and means by which those great faiths have
been, and are still conveyed to, and articulated and
steadied amongst mankind—why, then, to the end,
I must, and will, actually defend you against the sheer
distraction of such instincts and insights not actually
possible to you. But it is plain that you would be a
much richer, wiser, more developed and more grateful
soul if you could and did permanently develop the
insights and instincts that I mean. And certainly the
things I am thinking of — their perception — constitutes just the difference between a fully awake, a
fully educated mind, and a mind that is awake only
as to results, not as to the processes; as to what it
holds, and not as to who it is to whom it owes that it
has anything large and definite to hold at all.

You see, my Gwen, how vulgar, lumpy, material,
appear great lumps of camphor in a drawer; and
how ethereal seems the camphor smell all about in
the drawer. How delicious, too, is the sense of bounding
health, as one races along some down on a balmy
spring morning; and how utterly vulgar, rather
improper indeed, is the solid breakfast, are the processes of digestion that went before! Yet the camphor
lumps, and the porridge, and its digestion, they had
their share, had they not? in the ethereal camphor
scent, in the bounding along upon that sunlit down?
And a person who would both enjoy camphor scent

and disdain camphor lumps; a person who would
revel in that liberal open air and contemn porridge
and digestion: such a person would be ungrateful,
would she not?—would have an unreal, a superfine
refinement? The institutional, the Church is, in
religion, especially in Christianity, the camphor lump,
the porridge, etc.; and the "detached" believers would
have no camphor scent, no open air, bounding liberty,
had there not been, from ancient times, those concrete, "heavy," "clumsy," "oppressive" things—
lumps, porridge, Church.

There is, most certainly, a further difficulty in this
question. The Church, especially *the* Church in the
most definite sense, the Roman Catholic Church, has
at its worst done various kinds of harm, introduced
complications and oppressions which, but for it, would
not have been in the world. I know this in a detail
far beyond, my Gwen, what you will ever know. But,
my Dearie, let us keep our heads; and let us ask ourselves, not whether "Church" of any kind does not
open the door to certain abuses special to itself, but,
primarily, only whether *as a matter of fact* it has not
been through the Church or Churches that Christianity
has been taught or practised; that Paganism has been
vanquished; that Gnosticism and Pantheism have not
carried all before them, long ago: whether indeed it
is not owing to the Church and Churches—to the
organised, social, historical, institutional fact and
tradition, that the most independent-seeming, the
most directly inspired souls, do not draw a large part
of the purest of their conceptions. Thus George Fox,
the founder of the Quakers, taught that souls are
each and all directly taught by God, and have no

need whatever of Churches, institutions, etc.—all these
latter things are so much obstruction and incubus.
That he himself, at the end of two years of utter
aloofness from all men, was taught directly from
heaven (without any kind of previous initiation by
any human being) that Jesus is the Way, the Truth
and the Life; that God is Love; that to live is Christ
and to die is gain, etc., naïvely admits that, during all
that time, he had his *Bible* with him, reading, reading
it, all those twenty-four months. And how that, after
those entirely individual, entirely direct, utterly new
revelations, he *did* find teachings in St. John's Gospel
and Epistles, yes, not unlike his direct revelations;
but these revelations were *in no way* suggested by those
Bible passages, for these, Fox's revelations, were real,
were revelations from the living God to his, Fox's,
living soul—and how can something living be suggested by something dead? How can the Spirit be
tied to the letter? How can anything but God Himself,
and my own soul itself—these two working and
responding directly in and to each other—how can
or could they be otherwise than stopped or stifled by
anything not themselves—by any person or thing
other than just themselves in this their unique
intercourse?

Now all this does not prevent Fox from having been
a very spiritual man, and his good faith is transparent.
Yet equally clear is the utter rottenness of his psychology and the childish simplicity of his conception as
to the methods actually employed by God. For those
beautiful thoughts, those great facts as to God and as
to Christ, were they less beautiful, less great because
they had been perceived and expressed already

fifteen hundred and more years before Fox? And were
they less Fox's own, was he less free in uttering them,
because they had been awakened in himself, so utterly
freshly, by those lovers, thinkers and writers of the
past? Nor would it be adequate to reply: "Ah, well,
at least the individual Fox was awakened by, or on
occasion of, another individual, such two individuals
do not make a Church, still less does that one individual
(the Johannine writer) constitute a Church." Such a
reply would be poor indeed. For the Fourth Gospel
is already a *Church Document*—it already simply arti-
culates the faith and love of the Christian community
some sixty years after Our Lord's death. And even
the whole New Testament, or also the oldest parts,
even the unique life and love of Our Lord themselves;
even these again presuppose a Church, a community,
a tradition, etc., in which Jesus was brought up, and
which He learnt from and obeyed till He transcended
it, transforming and fulfilling all that was good in it.

You may ask, my Gwen Niece, what precisely I am
driving at? Do I want to make you a Roman Catholic?
Why, of course, no, Dear, I am busy, not with trying
to get you to turn actively "churchy" even. I am
hoping only to get you gradually to see the huge,
unique, irreplaceable good that you, as we all, owe
to the Church. Even if (which I hope may never
happen) you came to find it somehow impossible to
keep up as much of Church practice (Holy Communion, etc.) as, thank God, you practise now: even
then you would (if I succeed) feel a deep, deep gratitude to the Church—something like to, though considerably more than, you will come to feel towards
ancient Rome and ancient Greece. Want of such

insight and such gratitude towards any of these forces
constitutes always, I am sure, a very real limit and
weakness.

Farther back, I said that the main point to consider
was, not the harm done by churchmen at their worst,
but the special function and work of the Church at its
best. You see, Gwen, this is but the same principle
which comes continually into everything. Take *marriage*. What a unique means of training the soul,
how magnificent is its ideal! Yes, but nothing is, of
course, easier than to collect volumes full of instances
of infidelity, tyranny, non-suitedness, etc. A good
lawyer-philanthropist friend of mine has enthusias-
tically put forward the example of certain American
states which allow sixteen valid reasons for divorce.

Take *parenthood* : what a unique relation, what an
irreplaceable means for the mind's and soul's growth.
Yes, but the volumes full of misguided parental
affection or folly or tyranny! So with the *State*, so with
Art, so with *Science*, so with all that the hands of men
touch at all—hands which so readily soil even what
they most need, what is most sacred. But notice how
Church, State, Family, Children, the Marriage Tie,
these, and other right and good things, not only
possess each its Ideal, unattained outside of and
above it. No, no: they each possess within them more
or less of that Ideal *become real*—they each and all live
on at all because, at bottom, they are necessary, they
are good, they come from God and lead to Him, and
really in part effect what they were made for.

Now the four sendings of books, beginning with this
one, will specially invite you to note the action of *the
Church within the Roman Empire*. The present five volumes

deal with *the Church's Triumph over Paganism* ; the next
batch will deal with *the Church's Triumph over Gnosticism* ;
and the last two batches will deal with the hermits,
monks, and three or four of the largest minds amongst
the Roman Empire Christians.

As to this batch, read, my Dear, as follows:

1. Wiseman's *Fabiola* (a gift). The parts descriptive
of the Catacombs, Christian rites, etc., two or three
times.

2. Allard's *Persecutions*, vol. i. The Acts themselves
two or three times—the rest at least once.

3. Prudentius's *Cathemerinon*. I hope you will care
to learn some of these hymns, so full still of the sense
of all that Christianity had cost, and of how it was
worth, oh, all *that* and much more besides!

And 4. Then Allard's *Persecutions*, vols. iv. and v.
Allard will thus give you the beginning and the end of
those centuries of persecution. I hope that the Prudentius break will prevent the Allard affecting you
too much. You will sincerely tell me how it all goes.

I trust the Salisbury time will refresh and rest you,
my Gwen Niece. Kind regards to Miss Edith Olivier,
with whom I used to have good walks and talks
in Wilton.

13 VICARAGE GATE, KENSINGTON

6 May, 1919.

Your post card just come, crossing a long letter and
five books from me. I did not, in fact, explain in that
letter the following: (1) The *Fabiola* book, though not
actually great, is yet a thoroughly useful thing: it

was written after many years' frequentation of the
Catacombs, and much living in that early Christian
world. And it is thoroughly readable—witness its
translation into thirteen different languages. The
Allard volumes are very sincere, reliable, first-hand
work—better far than anything in English on the
same subject. I do hope you will love Saints Felicitas
and Perpetua—the sweet virility, the tender strength
of them! The Prudentius is, I believe, well done.
Prudentius is no genius like Lucretius or like Virgil,
but Prudentius is possessed by an insight and by
facts far, far deeper than Lucretius or Virgil ever
grasped. And he breathes a rich, utterly unsentimental
peace—because a peace after and in struggle, suffering,
self-oblivion.

Getting out all fine days now.

Uncle H.

13 VICARAGE GATE, KENSINGTON

My dear Gwen,   8 May, 1919.

Many thanks for little letter acknowledging the
Persecutions—books—and my long outpourings as to
Church.

My post card will have reached you later. I shall
love in due course to hear all your impressions as pat
and fat as you can make them. But this has nothing
to do with all that. It simply wants to tell you that
we leave this for kind Cousin Evelyn de Vescis,
Clonboy, Englefield Green—on Thursday—and stay
there possibly till September—and that we much hope
you will be able to manage a full week with us there.
In this I would read aloud to you, say, Browning's

great *Ring and the Book*—or some other amongst those
I want you to know, that you may happen not to have
read so far. And we could have thorough, easy, all-
round talks in that pretty Surrey garden.

P.S. Delighted you like Tertullian! Mind you read the
"Apology" very carefully—also the "Testimony of the
Christian Soul." But indeed all the treatises translated
in that "Library of the Fathers" volume are studded
with jems of thought, faith, love of the purest water.

13 VICARAGE GATE, KENSINGTON

14 May, 1919.

This, my dear Gwen, is only to say two little
immediately practical things. . . .

(2) I am delighted at your going to listen for three
days to Edward Talbot, whom indeed I know, and
whom I like and trust very truly. He will be able to
put before you a large, fine amount of that really
unlimited experience, wisdom, practicality, gained and
transmitted by the Christian Church. You will gain
much if you go simply without a touch of captiousness
—leaving quietly what does not help—using gratefully
whatever may, upon prayerful reflection, really help.

Pray for me there and always, Niece mine.

H.

CLONBOY, ENGLEFIELD GREEN, SURREY

My most dear Niece,   12 June, 1919.

I have been revolving your letter—its points—in my
old head and heart, and the following is the upshot.
I begin with the books and end with direct life.

1. I am glad you have read *Paradise Lost*, and still more glad that you do not like it. Rabindranath Tagore, at Vicarage Gate, told me that all his life he had wondered why Englishmen considered Milton a poet at all; for that to be a poet is not, primarily, to have a keen sense for poetical forms, but to be penetrated by a love of all things good in Nature, as vehicles and presentations of the spiritual realities—that an innocent sensuousness is a *sine qua non* for all real poetry. But that Milton is, in his heart of hearts, doubly cold, doubly hostile, to Nature—good Nature. That he is incurably a Puritan; and then has also taken over the cold side of the Renaissance. I think myself that you are more just than Tagore, and that those exquisite early and short pieces *are* true poetry, *are* innocently sensuous. I feel the same with *Lycidas* and *Comus*. But Tagore is right as to the poet in *Paradise Lost*—all but grand bits, such as the invocation of light, his blindness, the description of Eve in Paradise, etc. The fact is that Puritanism is neither natural (in the good sense) nor (really) Christian.

2. As to Shakespeare, he is, indeed, an utter marvel of richness. But in Shakespeare I always end by feeling a limit in a way the very contrary to Milton's limit—yet a grave limit still. Shakespeare is a true child of the Renaissance also in the *Renaissance's limitation*. He has not got that sense—not merely of life's mystery, etc.—but of the supernatural, of the other Life, of God, our Thirst and our Home—he has not got what Browning—on these points—has so magnificently. No dying figure in Shakespeare looks *forward*; they all look *backward*; none thirst for the otherness of God, they all enjoy, or suffer in, and with,

and for, the visible, or at least the immanent, alone.
When the soul is fully awake, this is not enough; it
only arouses, or expresses, man's middle depths, not
his deepest depths. It is not anti-Christian; it is even
Christian—more Christian, really, than Milton—as far
as it gets; but it does not reach the ultimate depths, it
never utters the full Christian paradox and poignancy.

3. As to the Martyrs, I well understand, Dear, that
you have had enough of them, at least for the present,
yet I do not regret sending you the Allard. I am
profoundly convinced that we can never be impressed
too much by the *reality*, the transforming, triumphing
power of religion—by the immense factualness. And
for the purpose, I know nothing more massively
impressive than those first three centuries of persecution. But it is literature, doubtless, more for a
mature or elderly man, rather than for a young woman.
And you will be able to feed the *astringent* emotions
(alongside of the sweet) in other ways. This, of course,
means that I hold these astringent emotions and
moods—this apparent hardness, this combat and
concentration, this asceticism, to be, in the right
place and proportion, an absolutely essential con-
stituent of the Christian outlook. Of course, a child
can and ought to have only a very little, and a peculiar
kind of it; a woman ought to find and to foster a form
and amount of it, different from a man's needs. But
where this element is not, there is not authentic
Christianity, but some sentimental humanitarianism,
or some other weakening inadequacy. By all means
return now, to Vicarage Gate, the three Allard
volumes.

4. I had got you your next parcel made up of books

about Gnosticism and the Church's immortal victory—
in the first two centuries—over that many-headed
monster, so live again amongst us. I had got passages
from the chief Gnostics for you in English; such
Pagan *Magic* writers and attempters of a Gnostic-
Magic substitute for Christianity as Apuleius and
Philostratus (*Life of Apollonius of Tyana*). And I had
finished up with Ibsen's grand, little-known play
picturing these last attempts—for those times—of
Paganism in competition with Christianity. I had all
this ready, again, to bring home the reality, the
irreplaceableness, of Christianity; and to protect you,
through the self-expansion we can attain by history,
from the Esoteric Buddhists, the Spiritualists, etc.
The Gnostics of our day, very small descendants of
those ancient Gnostics, who, bigger though they were,
could not prevail in the fierce testing of human life.

But I see you are hungering now, not for the knowledge of things to avoid, but for the further revelation
of realities to love. And so I am putting this Gnostic
packet away for the present. I will take it when we
have done the Pagan and Christian Greek things; as
a matter of fact, Gnosticism *was* primarily Greek,
though it broke out as a spiritual epidemic, at its
worst, in the late Roman Empire.

5. I send you instead, by Hillie for two nights at
Vicarage Gate, the following four books—two gifts
and two loans. Pray read them in the following order,
and with the precautions and considerations I shall
now propose.

(i.) The *Octavius* of Minucius Felix.

I think this is the finest Latin Christian pre-Con-

stantinian document, *as so much literature*. It is touching
and helpful also spiritually; but as to depth and power,
there exist greater things in that range of documents,
e.g. Tertullian. But then Tertullian is disfigured with
every kind of vehemence, want of proportion, bad
taste in details, sometimes even in great things.
Whereas Minucius Felix is so beautiful throughout
his form, that Boissier loves him for it. You remember
Boissier's fine analysis of the *Octavius*? Read, then,
this short piece, very carefully, ruminatingly, at least
twice—the Introduction first of all, and at the end
of the second reading.

(ii.) Turmel's *Tertullien*.

Turmel is an excellent initiator into Tertullian, and
will give you, I think, a vivid sense of what a genius,
what a dazzling variety, what a harshness and impossi-
bleness that poor great mind, that vehement, burning
and largely burnt up soul, was in real life, and is still
in his very difficult, largely repulsive, but astonishingly
live books, still. You will never forget, will you, Gwen,
that Rome—that official Christianity—deliberately and
continually refused to accept Tertullian's tone, or to
endorse his Rigorism? He ranks as the greatest of the
Montanist heretics. And most undoubtedly Rome was
right in all this, and Tertullian was wrong. Yet it
remains simultaneously true, that Tertullian's is the
first mind and personality of the first rank, classable
as Christian, indeed heroically Christian in intention,
that God gave or permitted to mankind, after the long
break since St. Paul. Our Lord, the Unmatched, the
Inexhaustible—God with us, surrounded by little,
little men. And then, promptly, one great follower,

St. Paul. And then a long break, followed by a second
great follower, Tertullian. And then a shorter break,
and a third great, indeed a still greater, a far mellower,
a far more fully Christianised Christian man, St. Augustine. You will at first hate Tertullian as much as the
Milton of *Paradise Lost* perhaps. Tertullian, a lawyer
by training, and a hard, fierce, African Roman by
temperament—with all the tendency to excessive
reaction and vigilant rigorism of most converts—
especially of converts from the moral corruptions of
that late Paganism, can seem—can be—along certain
of his most numerous sides—as legalistic, as mercenary,
as cold, etc., as Milton. Yet all this, surrounded by so
much more, and the whole as part of a personality
full of vehement *exuberance*—a personality which,
though it can shout unjust reproaches and apparent
arrogances, is, at bottom, pathetic in the sense of its
own unloveliness—so in his little treatise on *Patience*,
a virtue, he confesses at starting, which he, the vehement, the turbulent, never possessed. Please note,
too, that Tertullian stands quite unique in the way he
has always been treated by the official Church. A
man once declared a heretic, and his writings were
shunned by all but a few orthodox scholars, and his
writings would never be used with admiration and for
acceptance. But Tertullian was taken by St. Cyprian
as his, the bishop's, daily spiritual reading; and, indeed,
St. Cyprian's own writings are full of reminiscences of
those of Tertullian. And even in our recent times—
upon the whole more strict amongst the orthodox
than were those earlier centuries—this same privileged
treatment remains: there exists, e.g., a three-volume
Selections from Tertullian, made ready for sermons

throughout the Sundays and holidays of the year:
this by a French priest in the forties or fifties, with
full episcopal approbation. Why has Tertullian always
enjoyed this quite exceptional treatment? It is, I think,
not so much because he was the first to coin a whole
string of striking technical terms, which were taken
over permanently by Christian, especially by Latin
Christian theology, but because Tertullian's errors
were mostly excesses in opposition to the natural, the
first impulses of the average man or woman—thus
these errors were, upon the whole, harmless.

(iii.) Tertullian, English translations of some of his
chief writings, in the "Library of the Fathers," vol. i.

Although Turmel will already have given you well-
chosen, well-translated extracts from Tertullian, I
should like you to read, in this (very fine) English translation, the great "Apologeticus"—so amazingly rich in
vivid pictures and in vehement emotions—and the beautiful, deep "Testimony of the Christian Soul." I have
deliberately withheld from the packet a good English
translation of the "Testimony of the Martyrs" and
(again) of his "Testimony of the Christian Soul"—a
little volume like the Minucius Felix. I have so acted
because I do not want to give you a second Tertullian
volume, unless and until I find that you are more helped
than repelled by the fierce African. Of one thing I am
sure: no one can get much out of Tertullian unless the
person, man or woman, be thoroughly self-disciplined,
self-trained in the fruitful art and virtue of gathering
roses amidst thorns, and of discerning jewel eyes in a
toad's head. I want my niece to end by becoming such
a discriminator; how weary I am of the *lumpers*, the

whole-hoggers! I will not press you, over the Tertullians, as to the amount of reading of him. You may find even a single reading of the Turmel volume, as of the "Apologeticus" and "Christian Soul" in the "Library of the Fathers" volume, more than you can stand. Or again you may discover refreshing oases in that scorching desert, and may be drawn on by a genius, as certainly a genius as he requires bucketsful of expansion and of sweetness to render useful and palatable even thimblesful of his rigidity and bitterness. If you are thus fascinated, a double reading of Turmel, and a double reading of the English volume (at least of the two pieces proposed) would certainly not be too much.

(iv.) Palladius, *Lansiac History of the Early Monks*.

Gwen will think that her old Uncle has never done with astringency! My Gwen: just only you get inside any one of the deeper and deepest *men* souls, when fully awakened by grace, and you will perhaps marvel at, you will certainly have to note, the large presence—in very various forms, no doubt—of such astringency, so if it be only to understand the history of *men's* souls, a considerable acquaintance with such pickles and prickles, such salt and such mustard, is necessary. Besides, as to this Palladius book in particular, it admirably balances and completes your outlook upon dying Paganism and upspringing Christianity in the decadent Roman Empire. Also, you can hardly understand well the St. Jerome and the St. Augustine volumes, of the packet to follow, unless you know something about St. Anthony and his companions. I shall be interested to hear whether my little old Gwen

manages to discern, in these often strange scenes, a
necessary, abiding element (capable of all sorts of
forms and of degrees) of Christianity itself. There is
still a strange (at bottom childish) intolerance abroad
as to the ascetical element; but men—the deeper ones
—are again coming to see what they had far better
never ceased to see—so Professor William James, so
too Professor Ernst Troeltsch—both men of the largest
outlook. If you like Palladius, read him twice; if
you don't, put him by till you can appreciate him,
Dear.

6. As to worldliness—well, yes, my Gwen, it is a
thoroughly vulgar thing, especially when we remember
the *regal* call of our souls. There is, however, one
consolation about this—worldliness is a less dangerous
foe of the spiritual life than is brooding and self-
occupation of the wrong, weakening sort. Nothing
ousts the sense of God's presence so thoroughly as
the soul's dialogues with itself—when these are grum-
blings, grievances, etc. But, of course, the ideal is
to do without either worldliness or brooding. I say all
this, whilst confident that you do not class a right
amount of (and kind of) sociability and of pleasure
in it, as worldliness. Of course such social activity
and pleasure is right, and indeed a duty and a help
to God.

7. I love to think of the happy times you have had
in Westminster Cathedral and now in Salisbury
Cathedral. I take it that God in His goodness has
granted you the simple Prayer of Quiet—or, at least,
that you get given touches, short dawns, of it, now
and then. You know, dear, how much and often
I insist with you on the visible, the historical, the

social, the institutional. But this is done without even
the temptation to doubt, or to treat lightly, moments
of formless prayer. Such formless prayer, where genuine,
is, on the contrary, a deep grace, a darling force and
still joy for the soul. May you have, and keep, and grow
in this grace! What are the tests, the conditions of
this genuineness? They are two. Such prayer may
never become the soul's only form of prayer; formal,
vocal or mental prayer—the reciting of e.g. the Our
Father, the Glory be to the Father, Acts of Faith,
Hope, Love, Contrition (as in the prayer-books or
made up by oneself)—prayers, all these, we can give
an account of when we have done them: such prayers
must never completely cease. And such formless prayer
is the right sort if, in coming away from it, you find
yourself humbler, sweeter, more patient, more ready
to suffer, more loving (in effect even more than in
affection) towards God and man; given the first
(precaution) and this second (result) you cannot well
have too much of this prayer. And I think God will
lead you much along this path; and that you will
get beyond the worldliness, and other faults, especially
through it. For you will get to love it so; and it will
grow or will intermit, in proportion as you are faithful
in turning away from self. A homely heroism will
feed this prayer of speechless love; and the speechless
love will feed the homely heroism.

CLONBOY, ENGLEFIELD GREEN, SURREY

My darling Gwen-Child, 3 July, 1919.

Your two letters about the Canterbury Retreat were, and are, a deep satisfaction and joy to get and to ponder over; only our having three friends staying here, and my nights having, anyhow, become bad from doing too much, have kept me from writing at once. And even now I feel I had better not embark on your big learned questions—gnosticism and earthly progress, but I had better merely give you some impressions and suggestions directly connected with the effects of that Retreat or with the details of your coming here.

1. As to your visit here . . .

2. As to *Ring and the Book*, I had not realised the very happy fact that you knew it well already—you shall have the book from me here, but I think we had better not do more with it than just compare our choice of finest pieces. For I want to use these few precious hours to start you in St. Augustine in his *Confessions*. I have two precisely similar copies ready for this meeting; so you can follow in *your* copy what I shall read out to you from *mine*. I think this may well be the best way for you to begin St. Augustine, to do so with one who has tried to live the *Confessions* at their deepest these last fifty years—so stop till Thursday, Dear!

3. I so well understand both your deep helpedness by Edward Talbot and by the services; and, again, the dullness of the lectures on St. Francis of Assisi (entrancing subject though this be!), and your longing to get away from all that ladies' chatter. As to this

latter, it almost looks as if you had no rule of silence
(entire, or with but a break of an hour a day, say).
Yet this is a point so obvious and so important, that
I expect you did have silence, but only that the ladies,
even so, managed, over questions or the like, to get in
much dissipating chatter. Certain it is that at no time
is overmuch talking compatible with spiritual growth;
to learn interior silence, the not talking to self—our
little notions petted as our own, etc.—is fundamental
in the attaining of the spiritual life.

4. I especially understand the genuine, even great
pain that growth caused you, Gwen. A very good
sign. Truly, you understand, and will cultivate the
knowledge, of two facts or laws, Dear, won't you?
The first is that our ideal must be, in and for the
long run—a genial, gentle, leisurely expansion—no
shaking of the nerves, no strain, no semi-physical
vehemence, no impatient concentration—suffering and
(involuntary) strain may come to us; but all this will,
where good, be upborne and expanded into peace
and humble power, if we keep little in our own eyes,
gently watchful, and united to God in love. The
second fact or law is that nothing we may feel,
think, will, imagine, however spiritual, however *real*
spiritually, but has, in this our earthly lot, to be paid
for in the body. True, the joy of it will even do our
body good: still a certain subtle, unintentional strain
has been introduced into our nervous system. The
same, in its degree and way, would be true, if we took
systematically to music or to mathematics. There is
no necessary harm in this, and no means of fully
avoiding it. Yet, it is important we should be aware
of the fact. For such awareness will help to give us

a certain sobriety and moderation in all this our emotional life—a sobriety and moderation which will, if wisely managed, greatly add to and aid that fundamental Christian virtue—creatureliness.

5. And lastly—*consolation*, Dear, is sooner or later followed by *Desolation*; and the latter is, when and where God sends it, and we have not ourselves brought it on ourselves by laxness and dissipation, as true a way to God, and usually a safer one, than consolation. Day and night, sunshine and storm, union and aloneness—*both* are necessary, sooner or later, Sweet. But, of course, it is for God, for Him alone, to leave and to apportion these vicissitudes to each soul. And certain it is that it is of much help to have some older, more experienced soul handy also, who can and will, if and when we get into Desolation, cheer us on, by the reminder of the former consolation, and still more by the great fact that only through such vicissitudes— through fidelity in them—can we grow strong and deep in God and for Him.

Loving old,

Uncle.

CLONBOY, ENGLEFIELD GREEN

My darling Niece,   5 July, 1919.

As to Traherne, Vaughan, Crashaw (I add Herbert and Donne), I think they all contain much spiritual food—one could easily make one's spiritual reading for several years of them, if their form became bearable for long and extensively to one. Also there are single poems (e.g. Vaughan's "They are all gone into a world of light," and Herbert's "Sweet day, so cool,

D

so calm, so bright") which are perfect, indeed magnificent or exquisite—even *qua* poems. Yet the bulk of the
poetical work of all five seems to me hopelessly disfigured as to form by their quasi-perpetual straining
after some conceit, some play upon thought when
that thought's seriousness demands, in good taste, the
greatest possible directness, sobriety, simplicity; yet
again, if one compares them with real religious
English poetry, such as Keble, one finds, I think,
that they contain more sheer poetry than Keble. They
are more virile, somehow; I was sorry, in my last
letter, that I did not make a point of your ever dear,
fine father. Nothing could be more deserved than that
the thought of him should have been specially with
you in Canterbury; had he been frivolous and narrow-
hearted you might never have come to much!

Loving Uncle-Father.

CLONBOY, ENGLEFIELD GREEN, SURREY

From letter of 7 August, 1919.

My darling Gwen,

1. St. Augustine. I cannot exaggerate the gain
that I think you will derive from feeding for years
upon the *Confessions*. They, more than any other book
excepting the Gospels and the Psalms, have taught
me—and I believe they will teach you, will penetrate
and will colour every tissue of your mind and heart—
as to four things especially.

(1.) *Seriousness*. The average, conventional, latter-
day, enlightened, etc., outlook as to moral responsibility, purity, humility, sin, is just so much childish-

ness compared to the spirit that breathes in those
deathless pages. That entire way of recording one's
own or other lives, as though they were just so many
crystals, or at most so many plants; as though they
could not, in the given circumstances, have been
other than in fact they were: all that sorry naturalism
and determinism, with its cheap self-exculpation and
its shallow praise (because also shallow blame) of
others: all this is nobly outsoared, is obviously nowhere,
in that deep manly world of St. Augustine.

(2.) *Reality, Distinctness, Prevenience of God, our Home.*
This again, how little we are recognising it! And how
this fundamental fact pervades St. Augustine! It is because of this mighty fact (2) that fact (1) ever taken in
all its seriousness, leaves the soul rock-based, serene, un-
shaken; even though it wander far away from God, its
Home. Yet that Home continues ready to receive it back.

(iii.) *The Church, the Community, the Tradition, the
Training School of Seekers after, of Souls found by God
and Christ.* This great fact, overlooked nowadays as
fact, and the other two—St. Augustine had them all
three in deepest operation—each requiring, supple-
menting, strengthening the other.

(iv.) *Our Dead—ourselves when dead.* St. Augustine is
the finest antidote to our prevalent weakness here
again. What soul ever owed more to another than
Augustine to Monica? Can there have been many
souls more holy than Monica's? And have there been
many come back from more deadly sins and errors
than Augustine? Yet with all she was, with all her
saintly life and glorious death, all still vividly before
him, Augustine quietly records her frailties and prays

for her, and begs all who read him throughout the
ages to pray for her, for the forgiveness of her sins.
In this way even Monica becomes, if I may speak in
homely fashion, not a lobster-pot, but a springboard,
not a blind-alley or a terminus, but a starting-point
and a spur to seeing, willing, doing even further than
her, further than her whilst she was in this life.

2. *God.* I shall be glad if on this point you can and
will develop two distinct currents of conviction and
emotion: the *two together* will give you a deep growing
faith. By all means concentrate upon the lights that
may come to you, as it were incidentally, and as
background, in and through your prayers—of Church
services, Prayer of Quiet and Holy Communions; and
leave alone definitions of Him, and clear, reasoned
articulations of your faith in, of your conceptions of
Him. Good, excellent—provided you not only respect
for others, but you interiorly reverence as indirectly
but most operatively necessary for yourself, the great
positive conclusions of the greatest thinkers, theologians, saints, the great definitions of the Church
concerning God. I mean learn to shrink away from
the childish attitude of Schiller, in his epigram—that
he refuses to belong to any religion, because of his
profound religiousness, or of Goethe in his *Faust*—that
it does not matter *what we think* God to be, *what* we
say of Him—that it all equally affirms and equally
denies Him. I cannot exhaustively know, I cannot
adequately define, even a daisy, still less Puck. Still
less you. Does it follow that I cannot know, in various
degrees, really know, a daisy, Puck—you—that it does
not matter how I conceive them, that *this* conception
is not ever so much more penetrating, ever so much

more true, than is *that* conception? You know Gibbon's far too influential gibe at the Arian Controversy—that it was all a silly squabble concerning a diphthong— as to whether Christ was *Homo susios*—*same* substance with the Father—or *Homo sousios*—of similar substance with the Father. Gibbon thus confounded rich, far-reaching live differences, with their ultimate reduction to technical terms. You might as well declare that a controversy turning upon one million pounds sterling —that presence or absence was but a wrangle over the numerical sign—the vertical stroke—of 1. Since, on the one side, men wrangled "ooo,ooo" and, on the other side, men wrangled " 1,000,000." Of course all great issues can intellectually be reduced to such beggarly-seeming symbols; and in this reduced form they can only appeal to those who know them in their living fullness and operativeness. But it is a transparent piece of claptrap to decide off-hand, from such reductions, that this or that one is worthy of all respect because it covers great riches of fact, and that another deserves all contempt as a mere empty formula.—My Child will then just simply love and serve God in and through her prayers, her joys, her sufferings—her Church and her Communions—her children and her dear ones all—but she will *not* tilt at, she will *not* treat lightly definitions, however dry-seeming and abstract.

Two great laws—I am convinced they are—of and in our little earthly lives and probation. The one fact and law is, how unequipped are young people, say up to thirty at the earliest, for any final negative decision as to religion. I mean definite, institutional religion; and therefore how heavy is the responsibility

of parents and seniors if they provoke, if they give
ready occasion to, the young to any indiscriminate
revolt against such definite institutional religion. Such
seniors may have the deepest experience of what such
definite, institutional religion means in and for *their
own* lives, but they ought simultaneously to make
clear to themselves that this their own formed conviction has been an affair of time, and that they must
not presuppose it as extant in the young, or as simply
transferable to the young by command or even by
careful teaching. This, of course, in no wise means
that children and young people should not be taught
some religion, should not be wisely trained in *some*
religious (institutional religious) convictions and habits.
It only means that at every step you should remain
conscious of the inevitable, the right of difference
between these young things and yourself—and that
we will have gained a great point if they leave your
hands with only a little definite religion, but with a
sense that there may well be more in it than they can,
so far, see for themselves.

The second great fact or law of human life is that
good faith and the effects of our view and decisions
(upon ourselves and others) are strikingly incom-
mensurate. A child is taken over a factory—in the
best good faith it puts its hand into the machinery—
its good faith in no wise saves it from its own quite
sincere but entirely ignorant action. No doubt that
in more purely spiritual and moral matters, good
faith does more or less neutralise some of the effects
of inexperience, precipitation, etc.—but it does not
neutralise them entirely. All this then means that we
will strive to make the young feel more and more

Letters to a Niece

that *sincerity* is indeed a *one* most necessary virtue for them; but that *docility* is quite as necessary a virtue.

Your father exemplified this so grandly in music—the subject-matter of his special genius: he was not at all merely himself and sincere there; but for years he kept himself at school under Dannreuther, and to the hour of his death he was definitely learning from Bach and Beethoven, Wagner—was continuing enriched and enriching a great articulate and increasingly articulated tradition. Indeed, also in religion, I love to remember how religiously-tempered he ever remained—how nobly he overflowed and left behind him in *his actual* love *and interests*, such books as Buckle's, which, nevertheless (owing to that early, never directly revised inhibition and depletion), he never ceased from, now and then, praising to me. It was doubtless his most beautiful purity and love of young souls that thus kept him from being himself centrally determined by those brilliant materialists. And then, my Gwen— I look, not back, but onwards—not to what he was (even at his darling best), but to what he is, is in the true full life which assuredly he has already gained, or is in process of gaining.

My darling Niece-Daughter! I feel I know you, and God's purifications of you, much better since you were here those darling days. And I feel, as I felt at the moment you told me of a big, piercing fact, that you have all the materials ready to your hand of downright *holiness*. Oh, how kind and generous of God when He makes it impossible for us to become very happy unless we become very good. Bless you, Child. Pray for this old thing. I pray for you and the three.

H.

CLONBOY, ENGLEFIELD GREEN, SURREY

My darling Gwen-Child,   18 August, 1919.

I am always so glad when you can and do articulate some perplexity about one or other of the huge, rich, many-sided—not questions, but facts and laws which I try to help you to see—for thus I feel on sure ground —not only as to those great facts; but also as to your whereabouts, or your obscurity, concerning them.

I do not any more remember my exact object in telling what you have evidently remembered very accurately; but I will now take the point in (and more or less by) itself, and will make it as clear as ever I can.

You see, my Gwen, that with the all but limitless sway of *subjectivism*, especially since the eighteenth century, almost everyone nowadays, who is not deeply fed and filled by quite definite religious (institutional religious) life and convictions, thinks, if they think of truth and fact at all, of things not *given*, not found, but as things somehow projected, or created, by us (and this, all within and only for the purpose of our *human* nature and *human limitedly* human certainties and happiness). Strictly speaking, such an attitude should never speak of truth as in any sense ultimate and independent of ourselves; or of any reality as certainly existing prior to, and independently of, our affirmations of it. Such a temper of mind, if it talks of Church, of Christ, of God at all, can only talk of them as just so many "beautiful" or "interesting" ideas within your and my brain and heart—as things possibly without any reality outside of these receptacles. Such people could not ever raise the

Letters to a Niece

question as to *whether all three facts and realities* (as you
and I hold them to be) *themselves communicate themselves
to man—themselves invade his consciousness,* provided such
consciousness is pure and sincere. This question, note,
Dear, is distinct from the question as to whether or
not Church, Christ, God, are all three true, all three
real. The Roman Catholic Church—any and every
Christian group or individual—who would deny, or
even discriminate between, the truth, the reality, of
any one of the three, would stultify itself or himself.
God leads to Christ, and Christ leads to Church;
and, inversely, the Church leads to Christ, and Christ
leads to God. Or, better, the Church always involves
Christ, and Christ always involves God; and God
always involves Christ, and Christ always involves
the Church.—This, Dearie, is clear enough, isn't it?

But please note (not as contradictory to this, but
different to this) that when we speak thus we are
speaking of the complete interconnection, the complete three-mountains-chain, as God always sees it,
or some human souls here below always see it; as it
is in itself, whether many or few, all or no, human souls
see it. *We are not speaking as* (in this world of slow
growth, of complications, and of trial, of weakness,
cowardice and sin) *the situation actually stands.* Everywhere in this little "cabined" life of man we have
to introduce a similar distinction between the complete *type*, as most certainly willed by God, most
certainly planned by Him, and effected again and
again by and with His help; *and* the incomplete, the
merely inchoate *individuals*—always in all ranks of
actual life the considerable majority. I believe only
5 per cent of most *flies* ever attain to their full develop-

*D

ment; yet every one of these nineteen in every twenty
achieve, *as far as they go*, the type! They indicate, they
imply it. With *mammals* the waste is less, but still
very large—if it is right to speak of "waste" where,
very possibly, life is, after all, the richer for even such
inchoations. When we come to *man* we still get something similar, the many mere *beginnings* of human
life—children dead before birth, or before the age of
reason, idiots, the insane. Also the long centuries of
barbarism. All this, note, quite independent of any
personal fault, any sin, on the part of those inchoate
human beings.—Well, here again we can say that so
far (that is, apart from sin) the world is, after all,
upon the whole richer were there no such inchoations
than if it were reduced to those individuals who attain
to the full human stature.

Now this great fact or law, this great *difference
between type and individual, the realised ideal and the average
attainment*, runs also clearly through the manifestations of God to man, and the apprehensions by man
of God and His condescensions. The Jewish religion
was not false for the thirteen centuries of the pro-
Christian operations; it was, for those times, God's
fullest self-revelation and man's deepest apprehension
of God; and this same Jewish religion can be, *is*, still
the fullest religious truth for numerous individuals
whom God leaves in their good faith; in their not
directly requiring the fuller, the fullest, light and aid
to Christianity. What is specially true of the Jewish
religion is, in a lesser but still a very real degree,
true of Mohammedanism, and even of Hinduism, of
Parseeism, etc. It is *not* true that all religions are
equally true, equally pure, equally fruitful — the

differences are, on the contrary, profound. And it
is our duty never to level down, never to deny or
ignore, God's upward-moving self-revelation, God's
type-religion. At the same time our ardour requires
harnessing to patience, to a meek encouragement to
all the smoking flax, all the broken reeds, of our
earthly time and comrades, for these are God's
individuals.

Now then, back to your precise question. The
ordinary Roman Catholic scholastic textbook teaches
that such good faith (not adequacy), such individual
sufficiency (not type-fullness), is more operative with
regard to ignorance, or even denial, of the *Christian
Church*, or even of *Christ*, than with regard to denial,
or even to ignorance of *God*. This because, after all,
Church and Christ are historical, contingent facts,
which require to be imparted to us, in a way, like
the existence of the Emperor Augustus and the reality
of the United States of America, thus at the beginning.
But, no doubt, the non-Christian religions all furnish
their followers with (imperfect) conceptions of God,
so also with (imperfect) conceptions of Christ (Moses,
Mohammed, Buddha, etc.) and imperfect conceptions
of the Church (temple, mosque, etc.). Whereas God
is the metaphysical absolute Reality, which is involved
in, which indicates itself in, our deepest needs, thoughts
and conscience. When I told you that story of Monsieur
Littré, I did so, amongst other reasons, in order to
indicate how careful, how non-judging, as to individuals, we should keep ourselves, even where such
individuals ignore or even deny God. Yet I do think
that the ordinary Roman Catholic teaching is after
a very real distinction, and also that present-day

ordinary cheery dismissal of all thought of responsibility, and even of guilt, in such denials, is but part and parcel of the insufferable shallowness of Naturalism.

Devoted old Uncle,
F. v. H.

CLONBOY, ENGLEFIELD GREEN, SURREY

1 September, 1919.

I want this little scribble to reach you on your starting your packing-fortnight, my very dear Niece. I want to put very shortly, what has helped myself, so greatly, for now a generation.

Well—you are going to pack, pack and unpack, unpack for a fortnight. What is it that I would have you quietly set your mind and heart on, during that in itself lonesome and dreary bit of your road, Child? Why *this*, Dear! You see, all we do has a *double-relatedness*. It is a link or links of a chain that stretches back to our birth and on to our death. It is part of a long train of cause and effect, of effect and cause, in your own chain of life—this chain variously intertwisted with, variously affecting, and affected by, numerous other chains and other lives. It is certainly your duty to do quietly your best, that these links may help on your own chain and those other chains, by packing well, by being a skilful packer.

Yes, but there is also, all the time, another, a far deeper, a most darling and inspiring relation. Here, you have no slow succession, but you have each single act, each single moment joined directly to GOD— Himself not a chain, but one Great Simultaneity.

True, certain other acts, at other moments, will be wanted, of a kind more intrinsically near to God— Prayer, Quiet, Holy Communion. Yet not even those other acts could unite you as closely to God as can do this packing, if and when the packing is the duty of certain moments, and if, and as often as, the little old daughter does this her packing with her heart and intention turned to God her Home, if she offers her packing as her service, that service which is perfect liberty.

Not even a soul already in Heaven, not even an angel or archangel, can take your place there; for what GOD wants, what GOD will love to accept, in those Herst rooms, in those packing days, and from your packing hands, will be just this little packing performed by the little niece in those little rooms. Certainly it has been mainly through my realising this doctrine a little, and through my poor little self-exercising in it, that I have got on a bit, and Gwen will get on faster than I have done with it. You understand, Dear? At one moment packing; at another, silent adoration in church; at another, dreariness and unwilling drift; at another, the joys of human affections given and received; at another, keen, keen suffering of soul, of mind, in an apparent utter loneliness; at another, external acts of religion; at another, death itself. All these occupations, every one, can, ought, and will be, each when and where, duty, reason, conscience, necessity—GOD calls for it—it will all become the means and instruments of loving, of transfiguration, of growth for your soul, and of its beatitude. But it is for GOD to choose these things, their degrees, combinations, successions; and it is for

Gwen, just simply, very humbly, very gently and peacefully, to follow that leading.

Per Crucem ad Lucem.

Loving old Uncle,

H.

17 September, 1919.

Well, now, my darling Gwen, here is my letter for your restarting in Salisbury. I will attempt to make two, more or less new, points—very important discriminations—very clear for you, after first getting two immediate practical details out of the way.

I want you, then, carefully to study all the remaining Latin (Roman) Christian books I have given or lent you in the last packets. Tell me when you are getting to the end of this study (the little Tertullian and the Swete at least twice, please!), and I will get quite ready for the first packet of Greek books—classical (Pagan) Greek books first—on the same scale as that we did the Latin books on.

And the second detail is your proposed visit to Vicarage Gate—excellent idea! Hillie and I get back there on Monday next, 22 September. I have to speak at a Birmingham little private meeting—all my hearers clerics—on Monday, 27 October, and I ought to keep at least ten days free before, for preparation. Your Aunt Mary has a lady friend, who has asked herself till about 2 October. As soon after this 2 October that you can manage, say, three nights with us, the better, as the weather will then be more

likely to favour our getting our talks in Kensington
Gardens than later on. If you came by lunch-time,
and left by an afternoon train, that too would add
to our time in common. Let Aunt Mary or Hillie or
me know, some time pretty soon, Gwen!

Now for my points:

1. It is quite possible (it is certainly much the more
common state of soul) that your now deep and living
sense of religion is making non-religious subjects more
or less insipid to you—that you are feeling it rather a
bore to concentrate upon Homer and Pindar, after
Tertullian and the *Confessions*. But if this is so, or if
it comes on later on, I want you, my Gwen, *carefully
to ignore, and vigorously to react against, this mentality.* If
there is one danger for religion—if there is any one
plausible, all-but-irresistible trend which, throughout
its long rich history, has sapped its force, and prepared
the most destructive counter-excesses, it is just that—
that allowing the fascinations of Grace to deaden or
to ignore the beauties and duties of Nature. What *is*
Nature? I mean all that, in its degree, is beautiful,
true, and good, in this many-levelled world of the one
stupendously rich God? Why, Nature (in this sense)
is the expression of the God of Nature; just as Grace
is the expression of the God of Grace. And not only
are *both* from God, and to be loved and honoured as
His: but they have been created, they are administered
and moved, by God, as *closely inter-related parts of one
great whole*—of the full and vivid knowledge and
service of Him and happiness of ourselves. No Grace
without the substrata, the occasion, the material, of
Nature; and (in the individuals called to the realisation of the type) no Nature without Grace. Do you

fully grasp, my Gwen, what I am driving at? That
I want you, just because you long for religion, to
continue to cultivate, to cultivate more carefully and
lovingly, also the interests, the activities, that are
not directly religious. And this, not simply because,
"Why, of course, we must eat our dinner; of course,
we must have our little relaxations"; but, much more,
because, without these not directly religious interests
and activities, you—however slowly and unperceivedly
—lose the material for Grace to work in and on. When
we come to do the Church history of the Middle
Ages, and of the Renaissance, etc., I shall be able to
point out to you, on a huge scale, this great principle
either fructifying all or sterilising all. Meanwhile,
practise, practise it, Gwen; and keep it up, long after
I have gone! *Hardly any woman works her religion thus*;
but then, too, how thin and abstract, or how strained
and unattractive, the religion of most women becomes,
owing to this their elimination of religion's materials
and divinely intended tensions!

2. Hardly distinguishable in theory, yet rather
different in practice, is the other point I want you
carefully to watch. I have so much insisted upon
the Church in my recommendations that it may look
inconsistent if I warn you against Church societies,
Church newspapers—the little Churchinesses which,
I should think, must be fairly frequent in your cathedral
town—yet, my Gwen! just this, the equivalent of just
this, has been perhaps my longest, subtlest difficulty
and temptation, ever since, through God's mercy,
the Church took me, and I gave myself to the Church.
It was only when I was forty that this trouble and
uncertainty ceased—again owing to light from and

through a saintly leader. I never have gained the bigger lights on myself, except that way. To love Holy Communion, yet tactfully, unironically, to escape from all Eucharistic Guilds, etc.; to care for God's work in the world especially in and through Christianity, and yet (again quite silently, with full contrary encouragement to others who are helped by such literature) never opening a Church paper or magazine; and so on, and so on: what a pushing forward and a sudden inhibiting back all this seems to be!

Yet, if you are made at all like myself—what safety, what expansion, will be yours! This, though, only if you have your life full of good, wholesome not technically religious interests; and if these non-religious interests are more and more penetrated, warmed, widened, sweetened by the purest, humblest, most self-oblivious, homely heroism of super-nature—of Grace in the full sense of the word. Such a life will also greatly help you in keeping free from what might make you an unnecessary stumbling-block to other not yet religiously awake souls; and this without the least indifference or sorry "naturalising" on your part. At forty I learnt this; at forty or so, my Gwen, learn you this also.

I need not say that neither 1 nor 2 are of any obligation for you. They are only suggestions for you to watch and to see whether, and how, they fit you. If you cannot get forward in this fashion, by all means get on in the other way. I only want to clear away every possible half-notion that to love God, Christ, Church dearly, it is necessary for everyone (hence also for you) to be *churchy*. But again, Gwen, humility, consideration, patience: encouraging of others to become

quite different from ourselves; all this can alone
render the kind of independence I mean, safe, because
creaturely, and the isolation not fundamental or ultimate, but only one concerned with middle things, with
means and afflictions.

Am now weary. God bless you, Child. Be faithful,
and He will sweeten to you, in the long run, all things,
even bitter death itself.

Loving old,
Uncle.

VICARAGE GATE

My darling Gwen,   23 September, 1919.

Your interesting letter, awaiting my return here
yesterday, raises important points which I will consider with you in a letter a little later on (and when
you turn up here for one night), on 8 October. Better
that than nothing!

But I must at once make the following suggestions
to you as to the five books I send you to-day. Your
first Greek packet. They are all your property—except
one volume—Bury's *History of Greece*. You can, if you
like, begin at once on Homer. But I think it will be
better to take the three histories first, and only then
the Homer and the Hesiod. But in any case you should
read the histories in the order: (1) Bury, (2) Gilbert
Murray, (3) Croiset; and the texts in the order: (1) Iliad,
(2) Odyssey, (3) Hesiod.

Now as to these six volumes singly:

(1) *Bury.* I wish I could have found another one
volume, as recent and (for surface matters) as competent a history of Greece, by some other more believing

and spiritual writer. For Bury is a clever, smart, shallow thing—is growing it more and more, and aggressively irreligious as well. But this book is very much up-to-date as to excavations—the maps and illustrations are excellent—and in it he is not so rampantly doctrinaire as he has since become. Perhaps one careful reading with notes taken from it will be enough—keeping the book by you for further occasional use.

(2) *Murray*. Hardly, even he, a very deep, rich soul; but distinctly better than Bury—and has a wonderful penetration in the literature as such—I would certainly read him, most carefully, at least twice.

(3) *Croiset*. You will feel the charm of these Frenchmen; read it twice. Have got their larger five-volume *History*; and could at any time lend you this or that— or all the volumes.

(4) *Iliad*. I think this translation is the best for understanding Homer. Pray read and re-read it all, and compare the parts in the Æneid with the corresponding parts here—a very educative study.

(5) *Odyssey*. I send the translation of that cranky genius—S. Butler—because it so wonderfully hits off the homey tone of the original—and the maps, pictures, notes, are all most suggestive. But, of course, his contention that the author was a woman is sheer moonshine — not very unlike Harnack's contention that Priscilla (with Aquila's collaboration) wrote the Epistle to the Hebrews. But re-read the Odyssey and compare carefully corresponding parts (very numerous and lengthy) in the Æneid.

(6) *Hesiod*. Introduction and *Works and Days* at least

twice—remainder once—compare *Works and Days* carefully with Virgil's *Georgics*.

Devoted old Uncle,

F. v. H.

13 VICARAGE GATE, W.8

My darling Gwen,   6 October, 1919.

I write to-day, hoping that this (now the strike is over) may reach you to-morrow—on the first anniversary of your dear father's death. I often and often think of him; indeed he, just as you yourself, child, are in my poor prayers thrice every day. And I love to think that, if he, in that great life beyond, is allowed to know what happens here below to his youngest, he is glad and grateful for your deep growth during this year thus just gone by. This growth has assuredly preserved, and only still further deepened, the noble good — all the touching purity and generosity — he taught you and he exemplified to you, indeed which, in a true sense, he gave you with his blood.

I want to write now, also, because, since you cannot come just now (very naturally, though I am truly sorry), I should like to make some remarks upon quite a number of practical points or of questions raised by you since last I wrote.

1. As to the practical points:

(i.) Much frequentation of the cathedral. You know well, how greatly I love this for you. Yet there is one warning I would give you, and would beg you to bear in mind. *Do not overdo it*: I mean, do not take your utter fill, while the attraction is thus strong.

If we want our fervour to last, we must practise moderation even in our prayer, even in our Quiet. And certainly it is perseverance in the spiritual life, on and on, across the years and the changes of our moods and trials, health and environment: it is this that supremely matters. And you will, Gwen, add greatly to the probabilities of such perseverance, if you will get into the way (after having settled upon the amount of time that will be wise for you to give to the cathedral, or your Prayer of Quiet in general) of keeping a little even beyond this time, when you are dry; and a little short of this time when you are in consolation. You see why, don't you?—Already the Stoics had the grand double rule: *abstine et sustine*, "abstain and sustain," i.e. moderate thyself in things attractive and consoling, persevere, hold out, in things repulsive and desolating. There is nothing God loves better, or rewards more richly, than such double self-conquest as this! Whereas, all those who heedlessly take their glut of pleasant things, however sacred these things may be, are in grave danger of soon outliving their fervour, even if they do not become permanently disgusted.

(ii.) As to *Churchy* people, I did not, of course, mean devotedly Christian people, lovers of the Church, who work these loves into a large thoughtfulness. . . .

(iii.) As to Bury's *History* : please, Dear, write your name in it, and keep it as a further gift from me: it will be very useful for frequent reference in most of your further readings of Greek things. And, Child, try, by very frequent looking at the coin illustrations, to connect the chief Greek cities with their coins. It

is in that way that the geography of ancient Greece
sticks in my head. And dull as geography, and still
more chronology, are, when taken simply by themselves—yet without them—without a clear framework
of time and space in which to place and to remember
the facts, external or interior, of the history, you will
never remember the facts, and hence you will never
be able yourself to reason upon, to apply the history.
Let the coins help you very largely!

2. As to questions:

(i.) Shakespeare's *Macbeth.* I think you are right,
and that *there* there is a truly Christian penetration and
estimate. To-day week I will send you, on long loan,
a *glorious* book: Bradley's *Shakesperean Tragedy: Hamlet,
Macbeth, Othello, Lear.* You will love it, I am sure.
It is a book really worthy of its subject.

(ii.) Shorthouse's *John Inglesant.* I must say I feel
that book to have but *one* (a truly great) greatness, as
against three very bad faults — faults which, I must
confess, continue to spoil the pleasure I might otherwise find in it. The book, then, I think, has one perception, or, rather, an instinct stronger than the
author is himself aware of—I mean an all-penetrating
sense of the massiveness, the awful reality, of the
spiritual life within the Roman Catholic Church. This
that he thus sees, is assuredly a fact, and a huge fact;
but it is a fact unknown, or turned away from, or
minimised by the large majority even of religious
Englishmen. And I really believe that the undoubtedly
great fascination of this book for so many serious souls,
is just this its all-pervading sense of that very certain
but very largely unknown fact. But then I feel that

to one who, like myself, has lived within, has lived
and been redeemed and been formed by that great
life in that great Church, that discovery of Shorthouse is no discovery: if anything, such an one is
somewhat irritated that something to him so massively
plain, should—the discovery of it—stamp a book as
quite *sui generis*. And then, against that strength of
the book stand, I think, three great—even if smaller,
weaknesses. (1) The book, the man's style, indeed mind,
are *precious*—surely as much so as is Pater's *Marius*.
All that is turned and re-turned, is cooked—to my
taste to weariness. (2) The central figure and fate in
the book—Molinos and his end—are far from certainly
what they are painted here. *Possible* it is that Molinos
was innocent; I have studied the case very carefully,
and have said so in print. But there is no certainty;
and much—too much—mysticism and moral depravity
have certainly gone together in not a few other cases.
(3) The underlying doctrine of the book is very lop-
sided, indeed it is false. All through a Quaker indifference to the visible, to Forms, to History—to the Body
in Time and Space—is actively at work. Yet nothing
is being more clearly re-proved, quite independently
of the old institutions, by modern psychology, than
that that independence is only possible in a world
saturated with the results of dependence. Mysticism,
in all religions, always comes long after those religions
have won and trained the soul by their historic
happenednesses, by their close contact with time and
space. We shall find this, my Gwen, later on, with the
Ancient Greek, the Indian, the Jewish, the Moham-
medan, the Christian religions. And to think like
Shorthouse is historic ingratitude of a high degree.

I find that, throughout his book, those that insist
strongly on institutions and that fear or oppose more
or less pure Mysticism, are all, in so far, worldings,
power-lovers, Pharisees, etc.! Stuff and nonsense:
I *know* that this is a clumsy, false analysis; although,
of course, there are worldlings amongst the strong
institutionalists, as there are fanatics or moral deca-
dents amongst the "exquisite" mystics.

3. Dean Colet. Yes, he is a very attractive personality, and Seebohm's book is a good book. But
I have changed—I have had to change much as to
those Renaissance Catholic reformers these last ten
years. My ideal used to be Sir Thomas More. I still,
of course, admit their greatness; and I hold still, with
all my heart, that *that* Reform would have been far
better than the Protestant violences which supplanted
it. But I now have found in detail how profoundly
ignorant, how bigoted, were all these men, as to the
Middle Ages—they lumped these latter indiscrimi-
nately together, as just one long—six or seven centuries
or more — of utter barbarism and contemptible
puerilities. Dante and Aquinas, Anselm, Bernard,
the Poverello: barbarians! What a notion! The fact
is, certainly—we are all coming to know it well now
—that these men came at the fag-end of some five
generations of Iron Middle Ages, of their dissolution;
and they were too disgusted, too impatient, too much
blinded by the new light and lights, to pierce through
those 150 years, back to the Golden Middle Ages.
The Golden Middle Age is the culmination, so far,
of the Christian spirit as a world force and a world
outlook; and compared with its greatest figures just
named, even More and Colet, Fisher and Erasmus,

are thin and literary indeed. This too, Sweet, you
will be shown in detail later on.

Now I will have to be pretty silent till October is
at an end; have to incubate my address at Birmingham
on 27 October. Grand if you could come here soon
after.

Loving old Uncle,
H.

13 VICARAGE GATE, KENSINGTON

From Letter of All Saints' Eve, 1919.

My darling Niece-Child,

Here, at last, I come to speak to you again on
paper—the work, the getting to, and the resting
from, Birmingham have, till now, prevented me. But
I was very glad to get that sweet little letter of yours,
before starting off from this huge Babylon for that
also very big place. I myself felt, once off, that I was
attempting a great deal. Yet it all went off, I think,
quite well. My two forenoons there I spent in the
really beautiful Art Galleries—I enclose photo post
card of one of the pictures for my darling Gwen. But
how much of the art of not thirty years ago, or a
little beyond — Leighton, Burne-Jones especially —
has already died without repair, and why? Because
it was *precious*, unmoral, at bottom un-, even anti-
Christian (in the widest sense of the word). One feels
it affiliated to moral unwholesomeness. . . .

Strange it is, but a fact, that *human* studies should
more incline men to religion than *natural* studies;
strange because the difficulties against religion are
almost confined to precisely the human range. The

fact is, doubtless, that religion thrives, not by the absence of difficulties, but by the presence, by its offer and proof of powers not procurable otherwise; and that the need for these powers, and the evidence for the operation of their forces, only arises clearly at the human level.

.   .   .   .   .   .

Gwen, look up, look up with me, to-morrow! Oh, what a glorious, touching company! It is the feast of every heroic soul, every heroic act inspired by God since man began on earth. Sweet, how our little earthly years are fleeing by. Pindar called our life "the dream of a shadow." Yet in it, and through it, if we but watch and pray, and work and suffer, and rest in God our Home, we can find Eternity; that will never pass away. Pray for your loving old,

Uncle-Father.

13 VICARAGE GATE, KENSINGTON, W.8

My Gwen-Child,   3 December, 1919.

Here, then, is *Eternal Life*. I would advise your first reading up to the end of page 120, twice. Then, pages 303 to end, twice. And only then the far more difficult pages 121–302, also twice. Unless I greatly err, you will learn a considerable amount, provided you understand the technicalities as they occur. I did not choose the title, or even my subject; but you will find friends, already known, in these pages—St. Augustine, Huvelin, etc., not to speak of the Psalms and the New Testament—I wrote the thing praying; read it as written, Child!

I am sorry you are finding the Croiset so dry. I see why—my fault. Those two brothers wrote a delightful, not *dry*, *History of Greek Literature* in the five volumes— have got it. But I stupidly forgot how all abridgments are, almost always, dry as sawdust! So do not, Sweet, force yourself to read it through.

Your new packet is getting ready nicely. But the Herodotus is reprinting just now; and I have not yet spotted the Bury on the Greek historians. But I have a good little book on Pindar ready; Pindar translated by Ernest Myers, and a fine selection of translations from the *Greek Anthology*—if you don't love the latter well, you will show a patch of insensibility on your brain.

I well understand how delightful your father's Eton diaries must be; they will form an important part of the *Life*, no doubt. I love to note, Dear, that the same kind of spontaneous intelligence for, and thirst after music, and the same assumption that such intelligence and thirst are, must be, universal, are with you, his daughter, in reference to religion. Thekla has been telling me how marked she found a trait of genuine contemplation in you, Sweet. Well, it is all God's work; we will think of Him and love Him ever more and more; and we will bear as patiently as ever we can our loneliness in these respects. We will never feel badly lonely, if we keep expanding our direct knowledge of living lovers of God by a vivid realisation of the love of him borne in the hearts of souls now in the beyond.

I am so glad you loved the Huvelin: you will have noticed everywhere in him that tenderness in austerity, and that austerity in tenderness, which is the very genius of Christianity.

Must not scribble on to-day. Have started studying for my book, and I require oceans of rest in between.

Loving old Uncle-Father,

H.

My darling Gwen-Child,   2 January, 1920.

I had counted upon writing my first 1920 letter to you; but, alas, strict duty intervened, and forced me to write to other three people instead. But I want you to look upon this scribble as though written on New Year's Day itself.

I want, then, to wish you a very rich, deep, true, straight and simple growth in the love of God, accepted and willed gently but greatly, *at the daily, hourly, cost of self.* I have to try my little old best more than ever at this, now; for I find that any and all brooding or sulking or useless self-occupation—any pride or vanity at once disturbs or dries up my incubation-work. Professor James Ward and I agreed, one day, that nothing in philosophy, still more in religion, should ever be attempted in and with the first clearness (what, e.g., journalists are content with, and have to be content with), but in and with the *second clearness*, which only comes after that first cheery clarity has gone, and has been succeeded by a dreary confusion and obtuseness of mind. Only this second clearness, rising up, like something in no wise one's own, from the depths of one's subconsciousness—only this is any good in such great matters. And this process is costly, humiliating, and very easily disturbed by rubbishy self-occupations.

I am so glad you are trying to work the *Imitation* into your life: it is the only way to read it which is really worthy of what itself is so intensely alive. Now *there* is a book written as should be all religious books; they should be the quintessence of a long experience and fight in suffering and self-transformation. Also the twenty Huvelin sayings—they sprang straight from a life penetrated by God and the deepest love of Him. I will, a little later on, copy out for you another twenty sayings—they are all, please God, at work within me; and how happy, if they can get to work in the Niece-child also!

As to my *Apocalyptic Element*, keep it as long as you feel re-reading it can help you. I have two or three other papers which may also be of use to you. But, you see, with religious reading I always feel the situation is different from more ordinary reading. I mean that religious reading should always be select, slow, ruminating, and given to comparatively few books or papers. So we will, when you are again ready, get on with our Greek things—plenty of *them* —and, alongside, and behind them all, will be our few deepest readings, full of prayer, full of self-humilia-tion, full of gentle attempts gently to will whatever suffering God may *kindly* send us. A Jesuit novice once told me, with kindling countenance, how grand he had found the practice of *at once* meeting suffering with joy. God alone can help us succeed in this; but what, Child, is Christianity, if it be not something like that?

Loving old,

Uncle-Father.

FROM LETTER OF 17 FEBRUARY, 1920

My darling Child,   Shrove Tuesday.

I want this letter to reach you on Ash Wednesday,
when we all start Lent, because there is one little
practice I should like to dwell upon for a minute, in
case you have not yet waked up to it, or that you
require, perhaps, a little encouragement in it. I mean
the practice of some little voluntary renunciation.
I know well, of course, my Gwen, how much vague
and airy wisdom oozes out of the comfortable and
shallow modern mind about this. But then you see,
we have the *little* (!) examples of the Baptist in the
wilderness, with his wild honey and locusts meal;
Our Lord's Fast of forty days; St. Paul's mastery of
his body; and really, without a break, the asceticism
of all the great saints. I say this not to suggest anything
special in your food, sleep or dress; and as to the
amount of church, half an hour a day will be enough,
and it would be unwise to add to it, even in Lent.
But I am thinking of something without thinking
what—that would correspond, say, to my not buying
any books for myself during Lent. Depend upon it,
such little self-checks—checks on good propensions,
and checks self-imposed—where they spring from
love, really feed love. They are good things and still
useful to your spiritual growth.

                              Loving old,
                                 Father-Uncle.

13 VICARAGE GATE

My darling Child,   20 February, 1920.

You will by now have already got those two big

tomes of mine.[1] May you find sufficient that you
really understand, or can get to understand, to make
your study of them spiritually fruitful. The book has
been out of print some four years now; but this copy
is really (barring the wrappers) still quite fresh; it
was quite uncut-open yesterday; it is I who cut it
open for you, Sweet! Bishop Gore, who has been very
kind about the book, pointed out several grave defects
in it. That the style is often heavy, sometimes slipshod;
that there is too much of quotation, or semi-quotation
in it; and that the narration portion is without any
narrative charm. I am sure he is right about all three
points. But I feel him wrong about a fourth objection
of his: that I ought to have taken a fully normal saint,
like St. Teresa, and not a person so difficult to know,
so unusual, and more or less out of the way even in
her natural character, as is this Fiesca. He is wrong,
because I wanted precisely such a figure for my
special purposes. I wanted a heroic Christian who
was almost a Neo-Platonist, an Institutional who, in
some ways, hung loosely on institutions; a deep thinker
beset with much psycho-physical disturbance, etc.
Similarly Professor Boyce-Gibson was, I feel, mistaken,
when he wanted the book to have finished—the first
volume—with the death of Ettore Vernazza. He did
not see that I was well aware of the inferiority, at
least in charm, of Battista to Catherine, to Ettore.
What then? I was not aiming at a work of art, but
at taking in as much as possible of real life—to show
very original and exquisite spirituality having to live
on largely in this rough world, to get somewhat con-
ventionalified to suit the array of even very good

[1] *The Mystical Element in Religion.*

people. Of course, that Bishop Gore and Professor
Boyce-Gibson did not see these two motives of mine
in the book itself, proves how little an artist in words
the old Uncle is!

I think you would find the Appendix at end of
Volume I. too dry and hard for you. But I hope that
you will really care for, and learn from, the Introduction and the whole of Volume II. It is chapter ii.
(in the Introduction) that has had much the most of
the appreciation accorded to the book; but, for myself,
I feel as though Volume II. was the best of the whole.

My Sweet, you were thoroughly right about Richard
—his unripeness for Tiele—I am sure I often make
that sort of mistake for the young.

Your simile, your example of the two clearances in
musical execution is capital. So glad of it, too, because
it shows you are getting well into your violining again.
Am surrounded by the middle state—the obscurity
and muddle—as regards my book. One must just
work on and hope and pray. The God of light will
help us.

H.

From Letter of 5 March, 1920.

My darling Gwen-Child,

I was so sorry that you had a headache when you
wrote me that last note. Mind you do not use your
head on any concentrated work when you are like
that. . . .

But I was very pleased that somehow you are able
to resume the systematic non-religious reading. I was

a little astonished at this, having thought, regretfully, that your life had really become too full for such reading. This notion of mine explains that I was not, on the receipt of your note, ready with further Greek books for just this stage of your reading.

I wondered too, for a moment, whether you had not possibly forgotten, or had not yet explored, the *other* Pindar book I sent you. I got you this later booklet, just because I knew well how much the reading of Pindar becomes really enjoyable, the background of which you speak. I thought this booklet would supply this environment; anyhow I at once ordered for you an excellent book, *The Athletic Festivals of Ancient Greece*. But I learn it is out of print. I have now, however, gone one better and ordered you Whitley's *Companion to Greek Studies*, which will not only illustrate Pindar for you, but also the Historians, and the Dramatists, indeed the Philosophers also, I hope. I think I can count on having this fine book on Monday. . . .

The packet will contain three further books:

2. *The Extant Odes of Pindar*, translated by Ernest Myers; a scholarly piece of work which I should like you to read, ode for ode, each after the translation of Sandys.

3. . . . . a *Guide to British Museum Greek and Roman Life*.

4. . . . . a *Guide to the Principal Gold and Silver Coins of the Ancients, 700 B.C. to A.D. 1*.

When we have fully and repeatedly assimilated Pindar (mind you also read André Brémond's article on him) we will move on to the Greek Historians. I shall want you to get to first love Herodotus. We

E

will do him in a leisurely, sun-basking way which alone befits this leisurely genial soul.

I am sure that when, say twenty years hence, you look back upon your life, you will specially thank God for this double current I have tried to establish in your mind and soul. The current directly religious —this very pure in quality and genially costly; the current not directly religious, this also very large and deep—a great bucket of pure water into which to drop drops of the purest religious wine. This greatly helps us to escape all reactions.

Loving old Uncle,

H.

13 VICARAGE GATE, KENSINGTON, W.

My darling Child,   17 March, 1920.

I do not at all like these bad headaches of yours, and the suspicion that perhaps it is the fiddling that causes them. I should indeed grieve if you had to give up what so uniquely expresses your true self. I am comforting myself by hoping that, even if it really is the violining, it is *that* only in the sense that you are paying for the acclimatising of your nerves, etc., to this large, now new, life; and that, by dodging the headaches and wisely persevering in between them, you may be able to end by adapting your physical conditions to it—or again you might have to reduce the playing for a while, say, to two hours a day, instead of four hours. I hope that, in any case, my little old Gwen daughter will strive elastically to manage the fiddling after all. There is certainly a great art in managing one's nervous energy. I have myself, all my life, had to coax, and by various circumvendifuges, get my work out of my restive kittle-cattle machinery.

Glad Olivia does the types of Greek coins with you—I have no ambition for you to take up numismatics generally—whole tracts of that country seem to me hardly more soul-feeding than postage stamps. It is the *Greek* coins that really are educative—not as coins—but *Greek*, as part of that marvellous people's artistic creations. Had Richard here on Monday—looking forward to having him for a night soon. I feel you treat that very promising lad *exactly* rightly.

> Your loving old,
>
> Father.

13 VICARAGE GATE, W.8

My darling Gwen-Child,   26 March, 1920.

A hundred, a thousand welcomes, of nature and of grace, of the sweet spring country, of the future delightful garden, of the spacious, almost empty, bedroom—full, full, Gwen, of the thought, the presence, the real presence of the living God, and of the little old church so nearby, which will always welcome you to its sacred coolness and dimness, and remind you of God's condescensions in the Incarnation and Holy Eucharist! Welcome, too, from those nice, ten workmen—such an excellent experience for those three! Welcome, too, from those said three—how soon all three will be there, and how soon after they will have come really to feel this home at last, all the more so since they will themselves help to make it all really homey! Welcome, too, from Edward Talbot, the cleric

who has helped you so much and also will so much
care to see your *settlement*.

I am so pleased, too, that you have evidently got
fully bitten by Pindar, that that grandly clean and
religious mind is colouring your own. Bravo!

I received back from you, all right, the Gardner
Types of Greek Coins—the Butcher, the catalogue of
Greek gems (glad you admired that wonderful Augustus
cameo!), and André Brémond's paper on Pindar, and
my two articles on Troeltsch (I expect the poor little
Gwen found these really too hard to read). By all
means keep those other four papers of mine yet awhile.

I spoke on Tuesday evening last (23rd) to some
sixty students from all the English, Scotch, Welsh
and Irish universities and chief colleges. The Executive Council of the Christian Student Movement—
very eager, cultivated, religious young people. I spoke
for forty-five minutes on "Responsibility and Religious
Belief." Now I am busy writing out suggestions and
criticisms for a new sketch of that striking Sikh convert
to Christianity, Sadhu-Sundar-Singh. My chief desi-
deratum here is that he should come to realise not
only the utility, but the strict necessity, of definite
Church appurtenance and ecclesiastical subordination.
You see, a month after his conversion at sixteen, he
felt called to, and took, the vow of the Sadhu life—
the Indian ascetical, celibate, poor, wandering life
—which he now took as that of a Christian preaching
friar. He has faithfully practised this to now (twenty-
nine). But even the slight Church appurtenance which
sprang from his baptism by the Anglican Metropolitan
of India, and his six months' study in an Anglican
theological college, with a preaching licence granted

him at the end—even that he soon repudiated—to the great joy of the Nonconformist individualist missionaries of India. I am trying to show how crude, how without solid Christian precedents is such a monasticism, with such a sheer aloofness from every Church organisation. I am trying to drive home St. Teresa's magnificent rule for all her own life and for that of her nuns to this day—that she believed herself to have received very real direct revelations, and that she hoped her nuns might receive the same. But that *never* had she allowed herself, or were they to allow themselves, under the apparent suggestion of any revelation, to decide *anything* concerning their duties, work, appurtenances, dependants. On the contrary, the genuineness of the revelations, or at least the right use made of them, would always have to be measured by the *increased* obedience, self-oblivion, love of enemies, suffering—death, of the recipient of such favours.

God bless you, child.

H.

FROM EASTER MONDAY LETTER

My darling Gwen,   5 April, 1920.

I was so glad to get your first Old Rectory letter of 30 March. But first let me say that I have purposely waited till we should have got through these every year newly wonderful Church days—so as to be able to refer to the entire prism of many-coloured fact and emotion—which only thus together give us the true Christian reality and life. The great fact, and even

the commemoration of, Good Friday, would, alone,
be too austere, too heartbreaking; the great fact, and
even just the feast of Easter, if alone—even if they had
followed upon Our Lord's Hidden Life, or even His
Preaching, but without the Passion and its commemoration, would not have drained the Cup—the bitter
Cup—of the possibilities of earthly human life and
earthly human interconnection to the dregs. Good
Friday *and* Easter Sunday, the two together, each
requiring the other, and we all requiring both—only
this twin fact gives us Christianity, where suffering
holds a necessary place, but never the place of the
end, always only of the means. My great Troeltsch
always marvels anew at that *unique* combination
effected by Christianity—so earnest and so *un*rigoristic
—so expansive and so full of suffering without morbid-
ness, and of joy without sentimentality. We will all,
please God, see this more and more every year, that
these bitter-sweet, contraction-expansion, sacrifice
serenity, great days come round.

.   .   .   .   .   .

Oh, how, next to one's prayers and the practice
of the Presence of God, one's work, my absorption in
the mornings in my book—its immediate preparation
and composition, helps one to limit, to ignore and
bear one's load.

I am now deep in section 1 of the body of the book,
but dare not yet write any of this till I see more
clearly, more vividly, the main points and lines of
my position. It is *Kant* especially I have to master, as
to contend with—the section on him in *Eternal Life*
may have given you some fair notion of him.

13 VICARAGE GATE, KENSINGTON, W.8

21 April, 1920.

Here at last, my Gwen-child, I come to my scribbling
to you! I have four letters of yours—three of them long.
But I think they give me chiefly one big subject-matter
for consideration—the stress of dryness and darkness,
and what to do then. I know—oh, well, well—what
that means. And I do not doubt that with your special
temperament, such times must be peculiarly trying.
But—mark this well, Child—*irreplaceably profitable.* If
you but gently persevere through them, you will
come out at the other end of the gloom, sooner or
later, into ever deeper, tenderer day.

Let me give you three images, all of which have
helped me on along "many a flinty furlong." At
eighteen I learnt from Father Raymond Hecking,
that grandly interior-minded Dominican, that I certainly could, with God's grace, give myself to Him,
and strive to live my life long with Him and for Him.
But that this would mean winning and practising much
desolation—that I would be climbing a mountain
where, off and on, I might be enveloped in mist for
days on end, unable to see a foot before me. Had
I noticed how mountaineers climb mountains? how
they have a quiet, regular, short step—on the level it
looks petty; but then this step they keep up, on and
on, as they ascend, whilst the inexperienced townsman
hurries along, and soon has to stop, dead beat with
the climb. That such an expert mountaineer, when
the thick mists come, halts and camps out under some
slight cover brought with him, quietly smoking his

pipe, and moving on only when the mist has cleared away.

Then in my thirties I utilised another image, learnt in my Jesuit Retreats. How I was taking a long journey on board ship, with great storms pretty sure ahead of me; and how I must now select, and fix in my little cabin, some few but entirely appropriate things—a small trunk fixed up at one end, a chair that would keep its position, tumbler and glass that would do ditto: all this, simple, strong, and selected throughout in view of stormy weather. So would my spirituality have to be chosen and cultivated especially in view of "dirty" weather.

And lastly, in my forties another image helped me —they all three are in pretty frequent use still! I am travelling on a camel across a huge desert. Windless days occur, and then all is well. But hurricanes of wind will come, unforeseen, tremendous. What to do then? It is very simple, but it takes much practice to do well at all. Dismount from the camel, fall prostrate face downwards on the sand, covering your head with your cloak. And lie thus, an hour, three hours, half a day: the sandstorm will go, and you will arise, and continue your journey as if nothing had happened. The old Uncle has had many, many such sandstorms. How immensely useful they are!

You see, whether it be great cloud-mists on the mountain-side, or huge, mountain-high waves on the ocean, or blinding sandstorms in the desert: there is each time one crucial point—to form no conclusions, to take no decisions, to change nothing during such crises, and especially at such times, not to force any particularly religious mood or idea in oneself. To turn gently to other things, to maintain a vague, general attitude of resignation—to be very meek, with oneself and with others: the crisis goes by, thus, with great fruit. What is a religion worth which costs you nothing? What is a sense of God worth which would be at your disposal, capable of being comfortably elicited when and where you please? It is far, far more God who must hold us, than we who must hold Him. And we get trained in these darknesses into that sense of our impotence without which the very presence of God becomes a snare.

As to your feeling the facts of life and of religion complicated—*that* would be, I expect, in any oppressive way, only during such desolations. Yet I want to note this point for you—viz. that though I believe your *Confessions* and *Imitation* (with Psalms and New Testament), and the Church Service, do not strain you, nor, I think, my letters written specially for yourself, I am not at all sure of my writings in this respect. I mean that they are the writings of, I believe, a masculine mind—that they contain far more sheer thinking than is suited to a woman—even a woman with as rarely much intellect as yourself, Child. This is why I was slow to give or to lend you my writings. Yet I did so, because I want you to feel that there is also much hard thinking, much unpettifying of the great lesson which God's world and work convey if we can and do front them fairly. I wanted you, even in times of temptation, to feel the realities you were called to, perhaps straining at times—even apparently mere illusions—but not cramping, not petty. You can thus settle quietly into your little cabin with the huge billows buffeting you, the ship: their size has not been minimised: they *are* huge: well, God is in the storm as in the calm! But, of course, I am deeply glad the sunshine and calm are back again. And certainly these, and these at their utmost, are intended for our eventual life!

> Par passage pénible
> Passons à port plaisant,

carved a prisoner on to the wall of his cell, during his long imprisonment in the White Tower of the Tower of London. *That* is just it; both are true, both are facts: the *pénible* of the *passage*, and the *plaisant*—oh, its grand expanse—of the *port*.

As to Olivia's English literature—I enclose the list of *Selections* I was thinking of—from the 1913 catalogue of the Clarendon Press; they will be costing now, not fourpence but sixpence, I expect. Am so glad I was made to learn a lot by heart as a boy; Olivia might do the same from out of these excellent Selections.

Mr. Clement Webb is to preside at my address at Oxford on 16 May: so that I shall be sitting under an old and very tactful friend. My book preparations are getting on, and help me to forget the financial trials.

13 VICARAGE GATE, KENSINGTON

21 May, 1920.

Here I come at last, darling Child mine, with one of my longer scribbles!

First, as to the books sent this morning—four—all gifts.

(1) Herodotus—two volumes. The translation is

excellent, and the notes very good. You must get to
love, love that genial creature—a sort of prose Greek
Chaucer, a man with a genius for telling a story, and
with a deep sense of religion too. You will find Book II.
(Egypt) quite delightful, most interesting. Why not
do *that* most thoroughly, with Olivia? hitching it on
to the Egyptian history learnt at school?

It is, however, a grave error to treat Herodotus as
a genial old crony—where he describes countries and
customs seen by himself, and events lived through by
himself, he is *most* accurate, most reliable—e.g. Egypt
and the Græco-Persian War.

(2) *British Museum Guide to the Egyptian Collection.*
One of Dr. Wallis Budge's admirable books. Every
word is worth considering, with the pictures as
companion to Herodotus, Book II.

(3) Thucydides (mind that *y*, please!), *The Sicilian
Expedition.* This is perhaps the finest, certainly the
most rounded-off thing of Thucydides. Mind you
study it most carefully—twice every word at least!
The maps at the end, your occasional atlas, the *Little
Classical Antiquities*—the coin book. All would help to
make it all live and real—the only way to study
histories.

(4) Thucydides—the *Speeches* in Jowett's translation.
I should have liked to give you a complete translation.
But the complete Jowett costs too much for just now.
Besides it will be better if you first master the Sicilian
Expedition part and these glorious speeches. Later on
we can tackle the whole from cover to cover.

Of course, in the Thucydides *Speeches* you will look
out technical terms in your *Antiquities*, and before

tackling either Herodotus or Thucydides you will
read up carefully what Gilbert Murray says about
them in his *Greek Literature*.

Next as to Oxford. I was there three days. I had
much the biggest audience I have ever had—till this
I had 250 at most, this must have been some eight or
nine hundred. They were very attentive. I suppose
four-fifths undergraduates. Richard only three benches
off, smiling and most keen all the time; I felt it was
a great support to see a good many senior faces there
which I knew well. But, besides, I always remember,
on such occasions, what Socrates said so sensibly to
his disciples preparing for public speaking, that even
the biggest audience is, after all, only composed of
individuals and of small groups, whom they would
have no fear at all to address. Also I find it important
never to read, always to speak my things, to take care
to have humorous stories and not too great intervals;
and to manage little pauses, starting afresh in a different
voice. After the fifty-five-minutes-long address was
over, some two hundred and fifty people, almost all
undergraduates, came across to Queen's College
Common Room, and I had there, for an hour, to
answer some ten questions written down for me, from
the spoken queries. Only two or three were at all
good, I thought; but still such answerings do help to
drive points into people's heads. I felt it profoundly
un-Protestant, but was pleased to feel that its central
point no thoughtful High Church Anglican would
deny. It *had* an edge, but not against Anglicanism—
against Lutheranism; and yet I knew that at least
one keen Lutheran was listening, hoping, I am sure,
that I would turn out too superfine for the kind of

stuff, my Gwen, which I had to speak—if I would be truthful at all.

My last two hours were spent with Richard—who did the honours of his pretty little sitting-room very zealously. He went and bought for the tea a fine chocolate cake.

He looked such a fine, large, clean, straight lad, as he swung along the road by my side, without coat, hat or umbrella—in spite of showers—and only his gown rolled up round his neck and shoulders. I was a bit surprised to hear a "No" to all my games questions—cricket, football——

I get the impression of a considerable dash of your father—of his simplicity and impulsiveness—and of a streak of the Irishman, which, of course, he gets from his other side. A streak which tends to make him intolerant and absolute about people—and which might lead to breaches and conflicts. But the lad is clean and sound, and loves his mother dearly.

This time at Oxford has once more most vividly impressed me with the extraordinary greater happiness of the adult or even of the latter life—soul: the soul's life is, or at least can be, *then* so out of all proportion fuller, richer, steadier, deeper than any young thing can possibly attain. But how pathetic this makes them! I told them in my address that I did not believe humility was for young people at all. They, necessarily, knew, had done, had experienced so little—that they could not yet know their immense limitations and deficiencies. I do not say this of Richard—because he seems to me a modest lad.

Loving,
Father-Uncle.

Child of my Heart,   4 May, 1920.

Have just had your pathetic little lines. I too am
overwhelmed with work. And your and my work is
just the same, if we learn to do it simply for God, simply
as, here and now, the *one* means of growing in love for
Him. To-day it is cooking, scrubbing; to-morrow it
may be utterly different: death itself will come in due
time, but, before it, still many a joy and many a
training. We will gently practise a genial concentration upon just the one thing picked out for us by God.
How this helps! *How* greatly we add to our crosses by
being cross with them! More than half our life goes
in weeping for things other than those sent us. Yet it
is these things, as sent, and when willed and at last
loved as sent, that train us for Home, that can form a
spiritual Home for us even here and now.

The *Fioretti's* chapters are each complete in itself.
Five minutes would give you rich food. And didn't
St. Francis know such troubles as yours—bigger than
yours, and didn't he just rise to them in all transforming
love!

Of course, Child, I love you, as much, I do believe,
as though I were your bodily father—it is as though
that Great heart, your Father in God's other true
world, had been allowed, and had loved, to touch
my heart for you.

To-morrow I am sixty-eight, yet, thank God, I feel
fresh and young in soul.

FROM LETTER OF 23 JUNE, 1920

Child of my old Heart, . . .

The wise way to fight antipathies is never to fight

them directly—turn gently to other sights, images, thoughts, etc. If it—the hate—persists, bear it gently like a fever or a toothache—do not speak to it—better not speak of it even to God. But gently turn to Him your love and life, and tell Him gently that you want Him and all of Him: and that you beg for courage whilst He thus leaves you dressed, or seeing yourself dressed, in what you do not want to endorse as a will decision, but only as purgation if so He wills. It is an itch—scratching makes it worse. Away out into God's great world—even if your immediate landscape is just your unlovely antipathies.

Pray for your Uncle to become very, very humble— to disappear from one's own sight—with just God and souls; and one's little self one of these souls; how glorious that would be.

Delighted you love St. C.: *how* real she was!

Loving old Uncle,
H.

COURTFIELD, ROSS, HEREFORDSHIRE

Darling Gwen-Child,   10 August, 1920.

I want, though a bit late, to go over with you the points—the nooks and corners—of your Odstock environment and life. . . . And I want to finish up by a good story or two and some facts, that may awaken and amuse still further your anyhow lively three.

As to Odstock, I greatly loved seeing, actually living for a day with you, in that precise concrete time and space condition in and through which my child has to grow into Eternity and God—the Ever

Abiding. I so much cared for the Old Yew Inn, and
the genial old owner, who made himself very pleasant
to me as he drove me down towards the ever-graceful
spire of the cathedral, with his old, rather weary,
white pony. An excellent thing, having such a man
and such a conveyance for yourself and the children.
. . . Then I loved your room and, during that hour
or more I was there, I felt it was peopled with the
crowds of wholesome, peaceful apprehensions of the
Gwen-child. How it was here especially that Christ
and God helped and would help to turn isolation or
crowdedness, natural over-vehemence, pain, perplexity, pleasure and joy—all—all into gold, into love
of God and gradual assimilation to Himself. I was
especially glad to see that Crucifix there. Let people
say what they will, there never existed, there will
never exist, a symbol so deep, so comprehensive, so
realist and yet so ideal, of our august religion—as
just simply the Crucifix. I once read an address by
the late Dean Stanley, in which that brilliant super-
ficiality denounced the Crucifix as a mediaeval skull-
and-crossbones grotesqueness, and contrasted this
morbid extravagance with the poetry and smiling
restraint of the Catacombs and *their* symbols—Christ
as Orpheus, Christ as Good Shepherd, etc. As if the
admitted absence of the Crucifix there did not spring
from two very certain causes only—the fear of giving
the Pagans any clear clue as to which is meant for
Christ (lest such acutely hostile Pagans should thereupon deface or otherwise dishonour the image); and,
again, the fear lest those early, not yet traditionally
rooted Roman Christians, should have their faith
strained rather than strengthened by the presenta-

tion of God hanging on the (Roman) gallows—gallows
these (the Cross) which were employed only upon
slaves—runaway or the like *canaille*.

And lastly, child, I so loved your little dim pre-
Reformation church—so quiet and so devotional, so
placed as though made specially for Gwen. There you
can so well practise your institutionalism, your Holy
Communions; but also your special Recollections,
your Prayer of Quiet, and your praying for us all.
How I shall love it, if any keen trouble or deep joy
coming to you, you can and do run thither, whilst
it all is thus keen, to give it to, to share it with—God
—Christ! It is in that precise environment, by means
of those aids that you, Blessing, can and will become
deep and darling, humble and holy. There is simply
no obstacle, given God's grace and a good will, and for
these we will try and make our whole lives a prayer.

Loving old Father-Uncle,

F. v. Hügel.

13 VICARAGE GATE

From Letter of 31 August, 1920.

My own darling Gwen,

Here I have a fine lot of things to talk to you about.
Two from you and three from myself. . . .

I am struck too at how the little regarded, the very
simple, unbrilliant souls—souls treated by impatient
others as more or less wanting, are exactly pretty often
specially enlightened by God and specially near to
Him. And there, no doubt, is the secret of this striking
interconnection between an apparent minimum of

earthly gifts and a maximum of heavenly light. The cause is not that gifts of quick-wittedness, etc., are bad, or are directly obstacles to Grace. No, no. But that quite ordinary intelligence—real slowness of mind— will quite well do as reflections of God's light, and that such limitations are more easily accompanied by simplicity, naïveness, recollection, absence of self-occupation, gratefulness, etc., which dispositions are necessary for the soul's union with God. Such souls more easily approach action—and more easily escape activity.

.   .   .   .   .   .

A wonderful thoughtful friend insisted to me that the soul's health and happiness depended upon a maximum of *zest* and as little as possible of excitement. *Zest* is the pleasure which comes from thoughts, occupation, etc., that fit into, that are continuous, applications, etc., of extant habits and interests of a good kind—duties and joys that steady us and give us balance and centrality. *Excitement* is the pleasure which comes from breaking loose, from fragmentariness, from losing our balance and centrality. Zest is natural warmth—excitement is fever heat. For zest —to be relished—requires much self-discipline and recollection — much spaciousness of mind: whereas the more distracted we are, the more racketed and impulse-led, the more we thirst for excitement and the more its sirocco air dries up our spiritual sap and makes us long for more excitement. . . .

And that "side-shows"—*queer* things religiously—that what is not central, sober, balanced, may indeed still help certain souls in certain ways; but that, for ourselves, we should carefully eschew being drawn into attending to them, and thus weakening our *own* centrality.

But my Gwen-child will feed upon zest—and zest-bringing things, she will more and more become so central that even if she lives thirty years more than this old scribbler, she will be able with little or no human encouragement to escape excitement, lop-sidedness, oddity, etc. . . .

I write perhaps too emphatically because I am just now suffering over a very bad *lurch* of a woman I know well —a strange bit of sheer thirst for change at any price; of the weakness I have learnt sorrowfully to be prepared suddenly to come up against, in almost any woman.

My own first point brings up once more a matter we have often considered, but which I do not think we can ever get too much cleared up. A friend of mine, whom I have known for forty-five years, died some days back, at seventy-six—without any traceable shred of religion (at least in the ordinary sense of the word). He was a man of finely clean life, full of philanthropy, genuine and costly, a cultivated man, a scholar, also a man of naturally religious temper. It is certainly impossible to know the depths of any soul: yet certain points are once more clear to me, over this further case—that the agnostic tempest which roared between say 1855 and 1875 was so violent, that no wonder quick-witted lads went under, many, many of them. That even so, the finer ones managed to retain much that was high and right— even that was touchingly Christian—but that they owed this, not to Agnosticism, but to the Christian faith, the tradition from which they had broken away less than they themselves thought. And finally that, not only did they show faults or limitations—who does not?—but that these limitations were readily traceable to their Agnosticism. (I could easily draw out the details of this in my friend.)

. . . . . .

A matter of great delight to me just now is *a charming, most gentlemanly* and cultivated young Japanese, who speaks French and capital English, and who reads difficult German books with ease—a definite, indeed fervent, Christian—a Roman Catholic, who is finishing his training for a Japanese Government (University) Professorship of Philosophy. I am having a long talk with him once a week. He mourns to me over the intense materialism of his race and country, and evidently feels keenly the need for the whole poor modern world (aped by the Japs) to return to its senses—to God and the spiritual life as the true end of man. He wants to be helped find the best means of commending Christianity to such, at bottom, thorough Easterns. But I want to concentrate rather upon getting him to feel and to pursue still more precisely and vividly than he does, the special genius, the driving force of Christianity. I feel him that very, very rare combination—much intellect and still more soul! Pray for him, and for the Loving old,

Fatherly Thing.

13 VICARAGE GATE, W.8

4 October, St. Francis's Day, 1920.

My ever darling Gwen-Child,

Here I am, at last, once more scribbling to you! I have really not missed a single day on which I *could*

have done so. First, there was the getting ready for
Oxford—a big business, because one of us four paper
givers delayed everything by his absence abroad; then
returned to England to say that *now* (some changes
having occurred while news could not reach him) he
could not, and would not, join in; then let another
man write a paper in his stead; and then—when this
poet thing had actually printed his hurried contribu-
tion, paff! came back into the game and gave us a
(fifth) paper after all! Then last week was very full
with Oxford—our five little speeches, each one about
his own paper, and as to what he agreed and disagreed
with in the other four papers—this on Sunday, 26
September, with Mr. Balfour in the chair and speaking
also, when we five had spoken. *I* made the first little
speech, but spoke, I was told, too fast and too shortly.
Then came a French professor, a good friend of mine,
a fervent Roman Catholic. The little speech was excellent in its substance, but, it was generally thought,
too mathematically demonstrative in method and tone.
Then followed Professor S——, the man who had led
us such a life — able but very unsatisfactory — has,
somehow, quite lost the sense of what religion is, and
of why we so greatly need religion. Then came Principal Jacks, head of the Unitarian College in Oxford,
who, on our subject, "The Relation between Morals
and Religion," had distressed me, by printing in
his paper that a belief in a Beloved Community (=a
Church without God) was quite equivalent, as a
motive for morality, to faith in God. In his speech
Dr. Jacks was chiefly busy with that very vague,
Pantheistic thinker, Professor Wildon Carr, and thus
busy in a smart journalistic sort of way. And finally

came this Professor Wildon Carr—very thin, very
abstract, a good bit hurt with Dr. Jacks.—Mr. Balfour's
speech was beautiful. All morality, in the precise
degree of its depth and truth, consists in a continuous
and an increasing sacrifice of lower motives for higher
and ever higher motives. Yet we cannot, we do not,
make such great searching sacrifices for nothing, into
the blue. We make them, we *can* make them, only for
reality; and the highest motive, love, demands and
finds that Reality to be the highest possible Reality,
love, God. Hurrah!

It had been planned that then objections would be
raised to these six speeches; and that each of the six
speakers would have ten minutes for reply. But nothing
of this came about. For two Frenchmen now managed
to break in—the one to explain and defend the non-
religious moral teaching in the French State school;
the other to try and show that, at all times, the French
State schools had taught a Positivism. Especially this
last, a tiny little man, was interminable, and quietly
continued his exposition *twice* after Mr. Balfour had
pulled him up for being beyond the time allotted to
us all. This meeting lasted three hours. Then on
Monday and Tuesday I saw many friends and new
acquaintances, mostly connected with the Congress.
And then on Tuesday evening my great friend,
Professor Kemp Smith of Edinburgh, came home here
with me for two nights. The two full days of his stay
required all my strength for my talks with him—a
large, religious soul as well as a highly-trained intellect.

He said a number of striking things. That the age
of the largest spiritual mortality amongst men was
in middle life. That he had first been struck with this

when a great gathering of all its past and present students took place at Princeton University, U.S.A. You had to pass over the young men, some of whom, indeed, looked unsettled, uncertain, but not lost to faith and heroism, and to move on to the men in their forties: and, alas, how many self-centred, dried-up, all-to-pieces, cynical countenances!—Then what piercing insight into souls he has got! He talked of a cultivated, clean-lived ex-Roman Catholic priest whom I also know, and whom the average man would, I think, never feel to be anything but all right: "Why, the man is all to pieces: the wish-wash of the newspapers—progress, etc.—is all he knows or believes. All true insight is gone."—Then, too, this: "More and more I am coming to see that the chief source of errors is subjectivism, is distrust of, disbelief in, the natural, normal intimations of our senses, of our reason, of our conscience, of our religious sense."—And when I told him (brought up a Presbyterian) of how one of the members of our "Religion" Society had recently asked to be allowed to appear as a "D"—"Detached," because he had ceased to find any use whatsoever, for himself, in churches, sacraments, etc.: he, Kemp Smith, shivered as though pierced by a sharp instrument.

My Gwen: my doings have cost me a good deal: I know why. The fact is that like all three of my daughters, I have a very vehement, violent, over-impressionable nature, which, on such occasions, gets ridiculously over-roused, jarred, confused. Hence I have then a big job (quite apart from all visible doings) to drop, drop, drop all this feverishness, and to listen, as docilely as I can, to think, will and pray, with

only "la fine pointe de l'esprit," as St. François de
Sales and Fénelon never weary in recommending.
I tell you this, Child, because I am sure you are much
like that yourself, and hence may encourage you along
the same path of a most necessary stillness and peace.
The minute I at all attain to these dispositions, fruitfulness succeeds to fever. So with Gwen!

I have been thinking about and praying much to-day
for an American lady in far-away Chicago who has
been both comforting and alarming me by her entirely
unsolicited communications—three in number—that
she is the now fifty-three-years-old wife of a university
professor—a man of nobly clean life and spiritual
mind, but no definite religious belief whatsoever—
and mother to four children, of twenty-three, seventeen,
fourteen and seven; that till some two years ago she
herself was an Agnostic; that then, more and more,
St. Catherine of Genoa, in my *Mystical Elements*,
seized hold of her, and the instinct that she might
still come to believe much, if only she attained to
much humility and to much love of God's poor; and,
now, that she had fairly made up her mind to submit
to Rome to-day, on St. Francis's Day, she a Frances.—
Her very Protestant, touching mother-in-law was in
this my room with me, a week or so ago, to speak her
mind and to draw out my own.—Both to the daughter-
in-law in Chicago and to the mother-in-law in London
I said: that neither in that book nor in my life did
I, or do I aim at making Roman Catholics: that
would be odious presumption. That God and His
grace are (in various degrees, no doubt) everywhere
—but specially, very especially, in Christianity. That
the presumption is always in favour of souls remaining,

as to institutional appurtenance, where they are—it
being God's affair to make it clear to them if, doing
their best where they are, He wants them elsewhere.
That no æsthetic, etc., attraction, no preference are
enough: that only the sense of obligation in and for
the particular soul should decide.—The dear old lady
was very touching, but I saw quickly that even the
bare possibility that her daughter-in-law could be
seeking anything but services more gorgeous than
were those of the Ritualists, etc., did not, doubtless
could not, enter her head. So then I told her I had a
darling Niece who had found God and Christ and
Church—oh, so really; and that I loved to help her
all I could without a thought of her moving. That
I would gladly help, if I could, in a similar way,
with her daughter-in-law. Still, that we really cannot,
can we? become other people's conscience. The dear
old thing thereupon seemed satisfied with my declaring
that I well understood how *very* much she disliked
Rome; how sad and hurt she was, etc.—To the
daughter-in-law I wrote that my Niece had an Anglican
clerical adviser of a deeply Catholic mind, and more
spiritual assuredly than any but the finest (the rare)
Roman Catholic trainers. And that's true, my Gwen.

Loving old Uncle,

H.

13 VICARAGE GATE, KENSINGTON

My ever darling Child,   26 October, 1920.

Again late, but again not in fault as to this lateness
—brain gets feverish as soon as ever I add even such
a scribble as this to any considerable work—and my

work, or rather my jobs, have been considerable since
I last wrote. But I loved getting your second letter;
and you must never, please, await an answer from me,
if you have something further to say, and find the time
to say it in.

I am delighted you are about to get this, your first
real Retreat; and I do not doubt that you will be
greatly refreshed and braced by it.—No doubt, a
Retreat depends *somewhat* upon the Giver of it; yet
it really depends far more upon the simplicity and
generosity of the soul that makes the Retreat. I am
sure you already know well that you must evade all
straining, all vehemence, all, as it were, putting your
nerves into it. On the contrary the attention wanted
is a leisurely expansive one—a dropping gently of all
distractions, of obsessions, etc. "La fine pointe de
l'esprit," that is the instrument of progress, the recipient
of Graces. This old scribbler—how much of that
dropping, evading, gently waiting—as against his
interior vehemences and uproar, a sterile and sterilising restlessness—he has to practise! Yet the practice
shows him plainly (in the long run) that *that* is what
good sense and God want of him: peace and power
come *that* way and only that way.

I know too that you well understand that you should
never strain—never directly strive—to like people. Just
merely drop or ignore your antipathies. There, again,
I have been having hurricanes of antipathies—well, to
keep quietly ignoring all that rumpus—that is all that
God asks. And we then grow, through, and on occasion
of, these involuntary vehemences—they keep us humble
and watchful and close to God. I would suggest, too,
especially for the Retreat time, not to make too many

or too complicated resolutions; or rather, on the last day, to cut down the number of these reached by, say, a half. The remainder will probably be as much as you can wisely attend to *out of Retreat*, till next retirement.

The American lady is to reach London on Saturday night—30 October, and she leaves for America on 13 November. She writes from Paris and says she is much looking forward to talks with me. She is evidently a very genuine and sincere, but also a very unusual woman. She writes that she has no attraction either to God or to Christ—that in these directions she is perplexed; but that the one thing that draws and feeds her is the Church—the assembly of believers throughout the world. In Paris she spends as much time as possible in the churches, amidst the wor- shippers—that this somehow infects her with faith. She has all her life (fifty-three years old now) been an Agnostic; but this, somehow, breaks that spell! I tell her that very certainly the Church is for Christ and God, and not vice versa—very certainly. Yet that, after all, she loves the Church because it infects her with belief. Hence, she wants to believe, and delights in belief when it comes, and the belief is evidently not simply belief in the Church (is such a thing possible?), but belief in what the Church believes— in Christ, in God.

She did not take the move on 4 October that she thought she was likely to take. But evidently still *that* is in her mind. I shall, however, understand her case more definitely when I have seen her. I am proposing to her, our first meeting should be on All Saints' at early Mass, with a talk after breakfast.

My Sweet, of course *you* will be most welcome here on 5 November. We can, I hope, have a good talk afterwards.

I am so glad you begin your Retreat on All Saints' —my favourite Feast—the Feast not only of all the heroic lovers of God that have ever lived, but the Feast of single, heroic, supernatural acts, even if and where they remained single. May that darling glow, that genial sunshine of the saints, with Christ their King in their midst, deepen, widen, sweeten, expand, steady this darling little child! And pray for us all, Dearie!

Of course a second weekly Holy Communion would be excellent; but this must not be forced. God will provide reasonably easy means, if *that* is His will.

Loving old Uncle,
F. v. Hügel.

13 VICARAGE GATE, KENSINGTON, W.8

My darling Child,   23 November, 1920.

I loved your letter of 15 November very much. And now I must really try to answer its points, where these invite an answer, and to tell you the chief things that I have been learning from various happenings since my last.

1. I feel with you that a very big question is that whether or not to keep up your violin. Indeed, next to your elementary religious practices and attending to the children, I can find none as big. I am only sorry that it should have to be a question at all—you know

well how I deliberately put your non-religious readings *after* the fiddling. I could not give you a bigger proof of the importance I attach to that violining; for as you know, I believe much in the utility, *also and especially for one's religion*, of such an alternation of non-religious study. I have often explained this to you; and my life witnesses to its truth to me every day.

A pity that the problem has always to be "two and a half hours a day of practice or none." For you could doubtless get in an hour or an hour and a half without any crush. Yet I quite understand that it really has to remain at that alternative.

Well, I only hope much that you will, somehow, be able to retain the fiddling—those two and a half hours, even if it means no non-religious reading and possibly also the abandonment of one or other regular occupation besides. I am sure your music is worth it already, from its effect upon your happiness. So I trust you will be given light, not to abandon it, but how, without any dereliction of any real duty, to keep it regularly in your life.

And if Richard really takes to music for life and for his livelihood: *there* is another, big reason for keeping up your music fully.

2. I am very glad you are again visiting the poor people—I am sure you have real gifts that way. I have always much regretted that my deafness has so crippled me in that direction. I feel as if it would have done me much good, even though I am not sure whether I would have had gifts that way.

3. As to the Fénelon, I am ever so glad that you love him so. But indeed I felt sure you would. But I kept him back till now because I always fear as to him just

only one thing: that the reader may have too little experience of spiritual things to perceive, under all that apparent ease and suave simplicity, the masses of spiritual experience and of religious wisdom. But you by now have sufficient experience to bring to him, to perceive what lots and lots he brings to you.

Among the letters I feel that perhaps those which will suit you most and will teach you most are the letters to Sœur Charlotte de S. Cyprien. Oh, what a lot I owe to them; they are often, often gently ringing through my soul. The biographical "Notice" will have made you realise her as an ex-Huguenot—a woman of great mind and the toughest will, but naturally haughty, contemptuous of the average, requiring (as my Gwen-child does) to learn to lose herself in and for the average. If God, if Christ, loves men—and who can doubt it?—He loves *the average* very much—the poor little virtue, the poor little insight. How splendidly Fénelon feels in her a certain unchristian aristocratical-ness of mind—she was evidently a sort of Dean Inge in petticoats. Mind, Sweet, you bathe in, you saturate yourself with, those letters!

Then there are those letters to the two dukes (Che-vreuse and Beauvilliers): what grand direction as to how to lead a *very full* and yet a leisurely life! Do you notice there, St. Catherine's "one thing at a time"? And here there is also the insistence upon doing this one thing always with a certain environment of peace, of non-hurry around it. I find this double practice of golden worth; and, in getting up of a morning, I gently plan the day's doings, not too many of them for the application to them of Fénelon's treatment. (One has, of course, to be ready to modify one's scheme, as sudden, unexpected duties crop up in the day. But, even so, that gentle scheme is useful.)

Do you notice one very wonderful thing in Fénelon? It is the combination of a rarely light (not frivolous)— a light and elastic open temperament with an earnest will and gently concentrated determination. People as determined and as ardent as he, usually are, or become, heavy, rigoristic. And again, people as light and elastic as he, usually are, or become, frivolous and corrupt. By that combination—the earnestness without rigorism—he always strikes me as belonging, in his measure, to that minority of Christian teachers who have reached closest to that same combination in Our Lord Himself—to have caught up a few drops of that genial rain, that royally generous west wind, that gently drops and brightly blows through the virile sunshine of His love. St. Francis is another, and, of course, a much greater instance of that delightful paradox. The future of religion, indeed even already its present propagation in our poor old world, lie in it.

4. You are doubtless unable to keep on with the Herodotus, *that* may be able to come some time later. Oh, I love him much: he is so childlike, so quaint, so wholesome, a little like a Greek prose Chaucer, I think. And then his general tone is so truly religious; what a dread he has of all arrogance, and of its blinding effects and inevitable terrible falls!

5. As to Mrs. ——, she went off to America on Saturday, 13 November. We had four long talks, besides meeting twice in church. I think she will really persevere and will greatly grow, for she is deeply humble and very anxious to become still more so, and possesses a remarkable self-knowledge—knows

how to distinguish what in herself is a surface mood
and what is underlying, often very different genuine
substance. So on the evening of her first Holy Communion day, she said, with a mischievous smile:
"I trust and believe I shall never lose this my new,
fuller light: you see, I do not think I have ever felt so
Protestant as I have done to-day!" But I wish (it is
only a peripheral matter) that she did not put her
political radicalism so high in her scheme of things.

13 VICARAGE GATE, W.8

From Letter of 8 December, 1920.

My darling Gwen-Child,

I have to thank you for three very dear good letters
—as always very welcome and very carefully read. I
think the following points are those I see clear about,
or as to which I have facts worth reporting about.

1. *As to Fénelon.* I am delighted you love him so.
He is one of the, say, half-dozen of the non-Scriptural
writers who has helped me most directly and most
copiously in my own interior life—a life requiring
immensely that daily, hourly, death to self. I believe
that less keen and violent natures *can* get harm from
him; phlegmatic, drifting, inert temperaments could
take him wrong way on. But I doubt whether he
himself, the living man, ever harmed any soul he tried
to help, and he was too amazingly penetrative of the
particular soul before him thus to harm. The only
possible exception is, *I think*, his cousin, Madame Guyon:
possibly by his disciple attitude towards her, he did,

as a matter of fact, help her to become still more the
Quietist than she would have been without him.
Certainly it was for the purpose of covering her
exceedingly vague and wool-gathering expressions that
in his *Explications des Maximes des Saints* he strained
his own language, and got censured by Rome for
such terms. But then I have never taken him in that
livre manqué, but in these letters; and again in these
letters, as a man of immense action and persevering,
energising of will, addressing souls too vehement and
too intense, taken like this I have found him tremendously helpful. Do not hurry to return these four
volumes. . . .

I am sending you three other volumes of the Correspondence—the letters to his family and the mixed
letters. This because I have found that his helpfulness
was greatly increased by my realising him as a thoroughly flesh and blood, naturally faultful individual,
and as a man to whom God was not sparing of much,
much trial and purification. . . . They do, you will
find, humanise, concretise one's image of him greatly,
and here and there appears a letter, perhaps as many
as a dozen all told, which really *are* spiritual letters.
—Also pray specially notice and read and re-read
M. Tronson's letters: that good soul, the trainer of
Fénelon at S. Sulpice. Pray note Tronson's austerity
and *immense* ideal for Fénelon, and his piercing analysis
of his natural faults. A fine example of what I so
want my Child to grasp vividly, and for good and all,
that *usually* one thoroughly trained spiritual soul has
in the background another trained spiritual soul as
its trainer.

  2. *As to Du Bose.* I want you, Dearie, first of all to

F

realise that Du Bose is not—up to this his swan's
song—one of my men at all. His books are treated as
gospels by many young High Anglican clerics. But
they deeply dissatisfy me. Three ideas are with him
throughout; and I am very confident that all three
are gravely mistaken and highly impoverishing.

(i.) God and man are in the whole work of sancti-
fication, salvation, etc., on a *strict parity*. God's action
never extends farther than man's action. They are not
only *both* wanted in some degree: right! But they are
both, in actual fact, always and necessarily equal in
depth and in breadth. What stuff, what blasphemy!

(ii.) The possibility of Sin is a necessary part of
Liberty as such. In sheer thought, in the very nature
of things, to be free to do and be good, is to be free
and do the reverse—evil. No—and again *no*. To be
able to do, to be evil, is a defect, a restriction on
liberty. Perfect liberty always spontaneously, joyously
wills its own perfect nature. We should feel humbled,
not only by our actual sins, but already by the fact
that we can commit such things. (This alone cuts the
ground from under all the Byronisms as childish
unreason.)

(iii.) There is an element of potential evil in God
Himself. (This follows, of course, inevitably from
No. ii.) No and again No. You know how I try to
account for the existence of evil in the world, but
even if I were wrong in my particular solution for
the existence of evil—Du Bose's should be fought to
the death.

Du Bose has still further notions hardly more sound
than these. But these are surely enough. You will see

then that, not as a further specimen of a teaching I believe in, but, on the contrary, as a *first* pathetically late instance of a *sound* spiritual yearning in contrast with painfully reckless or at least inadequate theorisings, I have loved the strain (the strain more than the actual words) of this paper, in so far as it hungers for the Church.

By the way, the sad unsatisfactoriness of Du Bose's own all but life-long subjectivist Protestantism, helps me to see how little ideal is that abounding in its own sense of each of the sound currents of Protestantism which Du Bose even in this paper tries to make out to be somehow really satisfactory. In reality *each soul* requires centrality, inclusiveness, balance, sobriety, immense reverence. Its errors may get counterbalanced in the course of history and for mankind at large by the contrary errors, or its incompleteness may be made up for by the contrary incompletenesses of other souls. Well—but what about this soul itself? As to the particular sentence you quote as to the *Church as the only Christ* in which we are and we can do anything by Him and for Him—I think you have spotted a seriously excessive phrase. The Church is not Christ—is no more Christ than it is God. We require God and Christ and Church: each in and with the other. But it ruins the whole richness, indeed the truth, of the outlook, if any one of these—especially if the Church is simply identified with either of the other two. But there you have just a small touch of Du Bose's weakness, which in his books runs riot—he overstates till he meets, implies, the very opposite of what he started out to defend.

As to your own Church appurtenance. I want to say very

simply and definitely what I have long felt with you,
Child, but what I have, perhaps, rather implied than
at any time expressed *en toute lettre*—that I find God
in His goodness has given you a very—a sensitively
Catholic mind; that I never think of you, feel you as
a Protestant at all, but as an elementary, inchoate,
deep Catholic soul. I think you really seize upon
and feed upon those doctrines and practices in Anglicanism which, thank God, are Catholic, and there's
an end on't—and that you instinctively shrink from
what may be un-Catholic or even anti-Catholic there,
especially in the vigorous kite-flying which some junior
Anglicans somehow love to practise. The latter part
of the sentence means that I believe traditional High
Anglicanism—the stock that Edward Talbot springs
from, contains really but little that is not Catholic. It
is not complete, but it is, in its positive teaching, upon
the whole, most consolingly Catholic.

Now I must admit that when I began trying to help
you spiritually, I felt it might be my duty, or at least
the wiser course, to give you, and encourage you in,
not Roman Catholic books, but Anglican ones. This
might help to keep you from thinking of Rome.—But
then I saw, on careful examination, that I had no even
indirect intention to woo you for Rome, through your
spiritual reading. I simply wanted to give you the
best, the strongest, food for your soul. Was I really
to eschew what I believe to be best, simply because it
might indirectly awaken comparisons, misgivings, etc.?
As a point of detail I had thought of starting you on
Newman's *Parochial and Plain Sermons*—certainly classics
and well known to me. But then these sermons are
rigorist—how they have depressed me! Just the

opposite from Fénelon, who always braces me. And
really, I cannot allow you to be depressed—at least
I cannot organise depression for you!—But William
Law, and recently Dean Church, have written spiritual
things that are not depressing, and that, some time,
you might read with profit.—However, High Anglicans
themselves live largely upon the books I have recom-
mended to you. Indeed, I know some such who would
be indignant with me for not considering these books
as somehow really Anglican.—After all, you can and
will just feed on what truly helps you there to love
God and Christ, and to hate, and constantly to guard
against self. All this will fit in beautifully with your
praying in the little church—your Holy Communion
there and in the cathedral. I think your thoughts at
times about Rome as possibly for yourself probably
are a good deal a wish to be at one with your old
uncle. But I have already explained how truly I feel
ourselves at one. And short of a very clear light that
you *must* join, that it would be sin not to, you might
easily cross over and find yourself *less* at one with me
than now. Now you are getting the finest Church
teachings and figures in these books—and the weaknesses, the humannesses of Anglicans furnish a foil.
Then you would be environed by the poor *average*,
with *its* weaknesses and humannesses—very real there
also. — Hence I would have you, my Sweet, do
your very best where you are, with what you there
can get; taking care only not to fix yourself up nega-
tively—I mean against Roman Catholicism. Consider
it simply as what, even if the fuller truth, does not
concern you now—perhaps never will. After all it is
a truth which, in large part, you are living already,

and which you can and will live more and more, without any shutting up of yourself.

> Loving old Uncle-Father,
> F. v. H.

I was so sorry about the headache, but glad about the peace. Death and Peace—Good!

FROM LAST WRITING OF LAST DAY OF 1920

But indeed, above all, it will be your love of them in and for Christ—your love of and union with Him, which will keep or gain them for God. After all, every soul, boy or girl, as they grow up, have to pass through that delicate difficult crisis, when they themselves have deliberately to will the right and God. Even when the training and example have been perfect, and when the natural character is specially good. And, *of course*, it is your call to work for, and be ready, and be by, those three and their father also. From prayer and solitude back to them, and from them again back to it: and with them much in your prayer and your prayer much in them—*there* is a fine rich tension for you. Bless you, Child, for 1921.

> Loving old,
> Fatherly One.

13 VICARAGE GATE, KENSINGTON, W.8.

> 29 January–2 February, 1921.

My darling Gwen-Child,

I think of you as back at Odstock, and, in any case, ready for a letter. I have had to be a bit long before getting to this one, but have not a bit forgotten you, Dear. There are three things or four that I specially want to write about this time.

1. Your music. I still await light on this point. For, on the one hand, it does look as if the necessary amount of violin practice were straining to the head; yet, on the other hand, this music-producing is such a unique vehicle of self-expression for you. I should be so loth to see you give it up. The *crux* of the difficulty lies evidently in the *amount*—the *large* amount of practice necessary for your otherwise stiff fingers. If, say, an hour or an hour and a half a day were sufficient—that would not seriously strain the head. But then you seem to be sure that *that* would not be enough! I do not feel that the possible impossibility of keeping up that full orchestra for performances in the cathedral need decide the matter. For though it is, of course, specially inspiring to play thus in God's house—indeed in one of the old cathedrals—yet it would not, surely, be impossible—this failing—for your organist friend to get up chamber-concerts, quartets, in which you would be first (sole first) violin—concerts which, of course, could be for some solid charity, and which could be spiritually intentioned by my Gwen-child.

2. A couple of attempts to help souls seem to have gone awry with me just now: I mention the cases because you too will, sooner or later, doubtless yourself have more or less similar experiences. One was of an Italian man friend of about forty-five—an immense reader and somewhat intemperately speculative mind —a man who came back to Christianity, indeed to the Roman Catholic Church, from wildly secularist Socialism some eight years ago. I had built great

hopes of rare help for him from a Jesuit Retreat which I suggested his making for now about a year. At last he went and made one, the other day. But the priest who gave him the Retreat, an American, though a very good man, rather turned it into a series of theological speculations or discussions than that he kept it, and made it, into directly practical instructions in prayer, meditation, training of the conscience, discovery and reformation of personal faults, etc.—which is, of course, the direct object and function of a Retreat. I do not think those four full days have damaged my man, but they fed just his speculative bent, which I hoped would be starved, and have starved his devotional needs and chances, which I hoped would be fed. Ah, well—God may be offering him chances I do not see or know of. He is a well-intentioned man, and God will bless even unlikely-looking happenings.

Then there is a young English lady artist, who adored her mother, who had no religion, or who had lost what she had had. This damsel came to stay for three nights a few days ago, and to our surprised pleasure seemed definitely religious in her outlook (a thing which had appeared to us to be sadly lacking in her). And she wrote me so enthusiastic a letter about my *Christianity and the Supernatural*—especially as to my tact with young people—that I thought I could and ought to say something about religion to her, so I wrote her a careful answer dwelling on the importance of cultivating this her religious sense, just as she cultivated her artistic sense; on the great Jewish-Christian-Mohammedan tradition of prayer for the dead, which she might get into the habit of for her mother; and on the great importance of, whenever reasonably possible, only *preliminary* judgments. This last point because I had tried to introduce her to Browning's poetry—entirely unknown to her till I read aloud to her some six of his noblest easier pieces; and had found that she judged straight away and finally and with an angry hostility. As I pointed out, she could not, at that stage, know more than that, so far, she did not like him—after all, a very small fact, and one that might well be overcome on further acquaintance with writings which seniors of hers, well qualified to judge, had come to reckon of the rarest depth and richest delight. But this letter was answered by a curt, dry little note, telling me she had done all the things I proposed, now during several years. I was glad in a way, for surely even without any self-knowledge she must know whether or not she has gone to Holy Communion, often, indeed if possible every Sunday, and whether she has done at least fifteen minutes' spiritual reading every day. But then it was strange to note that she said "all the things," whilst it is clear that the suspense-of-any-avoidable-final-judgment practice had certainly not been done for several years. Ah, well; it does not follow that that letter was no use at all; and, in any case, one did one's little best.

3. Three dear friends have died since I last wrote—two of them quite old: fine old Dr. Alexander Whyte, the Presbyterian Edinburgh preacher and writer, a man with much of the Catholic mind in surroundings which made its utterance difficult; and fine old Lady Stawell (pronounced St*o*well), the widow of an Australian official, a sweet, strong serene Anglican, a devoted Christian. She had many a trouble; but her

*F

heroic resignation to God's holy Will, her generous
and strongly gentle application of her faith to her
entire life and dispositions never left her to the last;
and when I saw her lying dead on Sunday the countenance was indeed beautiful in its triumphant
spirituality. These two friends were respectively in
their middle eighties and late nineties. But the third
friend was only fifty; and *he* was carried off instan-
taneously by angina pectoris. He was a very devoted,
very popular, immensely active Jesuit priest—the man
who gave me hospitality in the Jesuit house of studies
these last four years at Oxford. He was essentially a
man of action, full of social service work. Well, *that* is
necessary too—necessary that some, with the gift for
it, should labour much at it. His devoted bulldog
Jimmy is sure to feel his master's death deeply: they
were inseparables, day and night.

13 VICARAGE GATE

5 February, 1921.

I think five to seven on the fourteenth will be best
for me—have me freshest for you. And Aunt Mary will
love to have you to tea at four-thirty. I would have
mine alone at that time, and we could thus start at
five, having satisfied our lower wants.

But this is specially to wish you a very deep and
devoted, a very peaceful and *épanoui* birthday. What
shall I wish you specially for the coming year—for
all the years of your life? I will wish you the ever-
increasing practice of just the kind of moderation,
alternation, mixedness, which you are already seeing

and practising. It is the moderation of yourself in
all things—especially also in your religion—and in
your very prayer; your always occupying a very
appreciable part of your clock-time and direct attention with not-directly, religious things; and this precisely because of, and for, God; to ensure stability,
sobriety, genuine detachment also, especially, in the
deepest things and joys. This practise and organise,
this make instinctive: and you will persevere to the
end, you will grow more and more spiritual and
holy; you will gain solid joy: you will become utterly
true and elastic and accessible. Even at seventy, in
such a life, "vainly the flesh fades, soul makes all
things new."

Holy Communion, for you, to-morrow.

Fatherly One,

H.

8 February, 1921.

I had intended, Child, not to write again before we
meet on the fourteenth. But I had forgotten that
already to-morrow is Ash Wednesday—Lent beginning!
So I write this little card to say that we will both of
us, will we not? make our Lenten penitence consist
primarily in the ever gently renewed dropping of
our several over-intensenesses, and in as gently and
really adaptably as we can, accepting, fitting into,
the rubs and jolts, the disappointments and dreari-
nesses which God in His merciful training of us may
allow or send us. And we will both add to this central
chief thing just one or two little renunciations. Am
dropping my after-dinner fruit and all book-buying
till Easter. You may be able to start some little thing

like that to-morrow. And for the rest, the darling poor, the open air, the Greek books, the dear dog, and any duty that may come to hand; all penetrated by your Holy Communions and an expansive, humble joy.

Fatherly One.

13 VICARAGE GATE, KENSINGTON

Ever darling Child Mine,   22 February, 1921.

I got your last letter yesterday morning, and though it was (as far as you yourself, your dispositions and affections go) as dear as ever you are, it nevertheless —through no fault of yours, but through much stupidity of my own—gave me grave distress and uneasiness. You see, as I have told you many a time, the biggest cross of my little old life which God has deigned to train by not a few trials, was when (all unintentionally, indeed for long quite unwittingly, but none the less really) I myself, so to speak, *put out my True's spiritual eyes.* I myself, who had chiefly trained her in faith and trust and love of God and Christ and Church, so strained and perplexed that very sensitive young soul that her very love of me and her natural openness to all impressions from me, bereft her for years of all faith—or at least of all peace, of all conscious faith. As I also told you, I had the *immense* consolation of seeing her come back fully, even before she married, of seeing with my own eyes in Rome, her darling, utterly, deeply spontaneously Christian and Catholic faith, love, life and death. She knew well, of course, how little comfort I should gain by any even of this, if there was in it anything to suggest that it was done in an attempt to please me: if what is essentially a free, self-responsible act and donation was performed even from such a touching but quite inadequate motive. Yet she knew, of course, what a unique joy it would give me if I could see here on earth my miserable blind work undone. And so, when she became just ill enough to receive Extreme Unction, she turned to me so darlingly, "Oh, Papa, what a grace, what a joy, to receive a further Sacrament of the Church." I knew exactly why she thus turned first to me. And then she pressed for, she got permission, to receive this Sacrament again, and was, the sweet, a little hurt that I did not seem to her as utterly assured of her love in so receiving it, as she wanted me to be, and as she knew I well could be. And so, of course, also with her confession, and above all with Holy Communion: but with these the evidence of her full return to the Catholic faith and practice had been before me for some eight or nine years. Now, Sweet: since my True died, I do not think I have cared to try and serve and feed any soul as much as yours. My chief prayer has been that I might never strain, never complicate, never perplex you, and that in a Fénelon-like self-oblivion I might just simply help and feed and carry you, if and when and where you required it—to let God lead. Well, Sweet, up to this last interview I think (with doubtless many little imperfections) God mercifully helped me to do what I believe He wanted me to do. But I suppose I was getting to count on my poor little insight or other highly-limited capacities, and it was time I should have a wholesome humiliation. I feel sure that this is good for me. But may I not have done any permanent harm to you, Child mine!

I mean: may I not have conveyed impressions so vivid that (however erroneously, they have so shaped and affected your mind) I cannot now seriously modify them? I will try, as surely is my clear duty, presently. But I want first to get three smaller points out of the way.

1. *As to health and music.* I am so sorry about the neuritis in the right arm, and the (of course inevitable) suspension of all violining. You will indeed be wise if you suspend or sufficiently moderate or modify whatever else may now tire or strain you. In this way you will soon get well again. And meanwhile you need not, need you? make any definite decisions as to the music. For I take it, that once in your average health again, you could manage an hour to an hour and a half a day without any marked physical disadvantage.

2. As to your mother's questions. It must be some twenty-five years ago that your mother once began to write me about some marriage matter—and asking some question, I forget what. I answered her as plainly as she had asked. And it tried me a good bit after, later on, when I found that she had told several of her friends about my answer—as very odd—as a sort of queer joke—yet, what a sweet woman she is—with such dear darling qualities! So, though I have, since then, been always reluctant to answer questions of hers, I wish her nothing but good, and would like to help her when and where I solidly can do so.

(i.) *As to the Virgin Birth.* I always find most help myself by dwelling upon the very early, the contemporary conviction of our Lord's sinlessness—something quite different and distinct from all and every other human holiness: and upon the consequent early feeling and belief that One thus sinless must have been, so to speak, the Beginning of a fresh creation of God, and cannot have been linked just simply as all other human children with at most only holy, in general sinful, never sinless, ordinary human beings. This is doubtless the deepest reason also for all the honour paid to His Mother.

(ii.) *As to the Eucharistic Bread and Wine turned into the Body amd Blood of Christ.* I take it that what repels her here is this apparent treating Christ as though He were divisible, and a divisible *thing*, and as though we literally ate and drank parts of Him. But any such notion is excluded by the very general doctrine of "concomitance" (=going together), by which, Christ, being not dead but alive, not a thing or things, but a Person: where His (risen and glorified) Body and Blood are, there also are His soul and His Divinity, each penetrating, and interpenetrated by, the other. The reasons why, especially in St. John's Gospel, chapter vi., the Body and the Blood, and the eating and drinking, are so strongly emphasised—is to ensure the very important faith in the strict and entire reality of Our Lord's Presence—a reality greater or different from His ordinary Presence in our hearts—a reality closely connected with the physical eating and the physical drinking of those species—the Eucharistic elements. *Of course* it is possible to have too carnal a conception of the meaning of this doctrine. Yet I do not doubt that—upon the whole—the danger lies far more in an evaporation of the Presence into no more than the universal Presence of Christ, or even into

a mere vague subjective thought of Him *as though*
present.

(iii.) As to the difficulty of caring for, and of fer-
vently attending, Matins or Evensong, I quite understand it, I think. But I would dearly love to see you
battle quietly against it, whilst using every reasonable
means to enliven your attention and interest. If the
services are somewhat long, yet their contents, especially
the Psalms are admirable. Why not get to understand
the Psalter *very* well? I mean not simply more or less
by heart, but, on the contrary, by learning to see more
clearly and more constantly the original meaning, the
first state of soul, in them. You will get in a few days
from me the late Canon Driver's beautifully precise
re-translation from the Hebrew of all the Psalms—
each printed on the page opposite to that on which
the Revised Psalter stands printed. I should love you
very slowly and ruminatingly to go through the
whole—perhaps slightly marking with pencil under
the words of the Psalms, in your Prayer Book, where
Driver has taught you the precise original meaning
where the Prayer Book text is obscure. This would
bring rich life and deep feeling into them, or rather
would reveal to you the life and the feeling. Our own
Mass and Benediction, and especially Vespers and
Compline, are, of course, filled with various Psalms.
So also for understanding our, the great old Latin
services, a sound knowledge of the Psalter is very
useful. Then I look forward to the days, off and on,
when with others, you would have a companion at
these services. This would break and limit the
isolation a good bit. . . .

These difficulties are all so many additional special

reasons for your holding out, even if you mostly have
to go alone. But, Sweet, you would, of course, practise
moderation in the matter; going, as you do, to Holy
Communion at least once a week, and praying by
yourself, as you do, in your little church by yourself.
I do not see that you need have more than Evensong
on the Sundays: that is supposing you get Holy
Communion *every* Sunday morning.

And now at last I come to the biggest thing in your
letter: what you say about liberty, freedom, in the
Roman Catholic Church. I sadly realise that, given
my remarks, or rather given the sheer fact of my
raising the point to you at all the other day, you
could not—at least if you followed me then in your
usual sweetly receptive way—think at all differently.
For if your own freedom would not, by becoming a
Roman Catholic, get curtailed, where would be the
object of my raising the point to you at all? It *must*
have concerned yourself; and if it did not concern
you, where lies the excess in your conclusion, from,
indeed in, your simple reproduction of my words?
I see this quite plainly, Child. But I soon felt very
uncomfortable, you gone, as to what I had said.
I know I spoke with edge and concentration, and
I have waited anxiously to see its reception by you.
Be a dear child now, and drop what I said then,
attending simply to what I will write now.

First then, there can be no serious question of any
curtailment of any right and reasonable freedom—
such freedom as you practise now in your reading,
studying, thinking—if ever you became a Roman
Catholic. I have deliberately gone through all the
duties, all even the chances and influences that would

then surround you, and I can discover no such curtailment, either certain, or even probable.—Of course,
you would yourself have a wide choice of confessors,
devotions, spiritual books, religious habits; and if you
yourself chose, or you let yourself go to vehement
reaction against all your past, even where (as, thank
God, it is) very good and wise: you could work your
appurtenance to the Church in an impoverishing
way. But that would be your own doing; and already
you see far too plainly how central must always be
and remain the dropping of all excess and vehemence, for such a danger to be at all near or likely.
If you were a man, and a critical historian and
philosophical thinker, and these activities occupied
with religion, not simply reproductive or selective,
but original and reconstructive, the question of freedom would occur. But note, my Sweet, that not only
it does not—it really does not—occur for yourself: it gets
answered by me, with whom it does, it cannot but
occur, in the sense opposite to that in which you
answer it for yourself. I deliberately admit *some*
difficulty, *some* complication for such as myself; but
I do not cease, thank God, to see and experience that
the gain of my Roman Catholic appurtenance is, even
simply for the solidity of my freedom, for the balance
and reality of my outlook—*just simply even to my life
of scholarship and thinking* IMMENSE. I know it is. So that
I am sure that you are doubly removed from any
real curtailment of your liberty, if ever you came to
the Roman Catholic Church: for you are not a scholar,
a thinker, by profession—and, even if you were, you
could, and ought, and would gain a depth *and breadth*
of rich liberty beyond what you could acquire else-

where. You can see that, as to men like myself, this is my real conviction. How else could you explain my always keeping open in my mind the possibility and desirableness of Professor Norman Kemp Smith, of Edinburgh, coming to us later on?

Do not, Sweet, misunderstand any of this as a plea, as even the most indirect pressure for your changing. No: it has nothing to do with *that*. Only deep, strong, most clear calls of conscience would make it right for you to think of such a change. I only want, if God will bless this old bungler, to remove a false impression—I do not want, if ever such a condition of conscience arose, for you to be stopped from following it up by a *bugbear*, alas, of my own suscitation. You will, Blessing, if you truly can say so, give me an immense relief by telling me that you now understand. I will, of course, gladly explain further, if there is anything seriously obscure. I see that there was a double self-seeking about me that evening. I was thinking of my own case, instead of yours—and I was thinking of my own case unmanfully, softly, complainingly. As a matter of fact I have found, and I have at this moment, masses of deepest sympathy, even of a purely personal kind, and this not simply from dry scholars, but from darling Catholic saints of God. If I got more, it would turn my old head.

And now, my Child, one good hug, and another good hug, and a third good hug. And Christ bless you, guard you, expand, pacify, and give you genial joy, here, now, and for ever.

Loving old Fatherly One,

H.

13 VICARAGE GATE

28 February, 1921.

Delighted by your letter and will now try and drop all that distress on that point from my mind. Of course you may copy parts or all of that L.S.S.R. paper of mine. You have never mentioned receiving a proof of a review of mine of a book by Heiler on *Prayer*. You are meant to keep *that*. As to St. Francis de Sales, I will send you some. Perhaps his chief work at once, the *Traité de L'Amour de Dieu*. I somewhat fear your finding him a bit cloying. I hope you will not, for his substance is admirable. How many souls he has trained to sanctity! But I want you still to read two short Fénelons—his *Education des Filles* and his chaplain's account of his daily life at Cambrai—the man lives there before one. Also Shakespeare—I too place *Macbeth* highest for spiritual insight—though *Lear* I take to be one of the most awful evidences of power of all three tragedies. But I like to keep the four tragedies compared—surely *Othello* stands almost as high spiritually as *Macbeth*?

F. v. H.

13 VICARAGE GATE, W.8

1 March, 1921.

Still tied to bedroom, but was able this morning to finish selection of Old Testament passages for my book.

Once and again was immensely struck and impressed with the richness, reality, penetrating spirituality of the Psalter, the Psalms at their best, a pity that frequent use—imperfect translation—and the backward elements (vindictiveness, earthly rewards—nebulousness as to the other life) so largely obscure these very magnificent things.—Will have a lovely Easter book to suggest.

4 March. Still in bedroom—the obstinate chest cold and cough upon the whole better, but still far from gone. Worst is, that not getting out leaves brain extra wearyable.

Thanks for Fénelon returned. Glad you are keeping the *Lettres Spirituelles* a bit. What utterly alive things they are! Like all the finest results of immense training, cost, perseverance, grace, they stand there as though they could not be otherwise—as if anyone, everyone thought it all!

Have just accepted to speak at a large Summer School at Swanwick on Sunday, 3 July.—Will try to get them to accept some quite definite point for my discourse.

13 VICARAGE GATE, W.8

Child of my old Heart,   11 April, 1921.

Here is your book back. If you re-read your copy of my (Notes) on Holy Communion you will find it much more intelligible, I am sure. You had copied carefully, but my poor text was rough!

Dare not write properly till after 2 May, as I explained on post card.—But one or two post cards will, perhaps, get written, and I can, of course, always gladly read letters from you. Everything, *everything* at once, sweetened in the love of God—of Christ.

> que rien ne t' épouvante,
> que rien ne te trouble;
> Tout passe;
> Dieu seul.

S. Teresa.

What jolly good stuff those saints give one, don't they?

Loving old Uncle-Father,

H.

13 VICARAGE GATE, KENSINGTON, W.8

Ascension Day, 5 May, 1921.

Here at last I am more free again, and the first letter I write because I love to write it, is to my most dear little old Thing—though really "little," at least physically! is not the right word.

It was only late on Thursday night, 3rd, that the big strain came to an end, through the delivery of my address on "Suffering in God." The thing was, as it were, externally a success: twenty-six of us met together—a large number for our not large society. And they were all, as ever, most kind and dear to me personally. But I trust it is sincerely so—one feels, on such occasions, more cheered by agreement in the convictions expressed, than by any amount of such pleasant attentions. Some twelve of my listeners spoke through my machine after and on the paper; and only two agreed with my fundamental—to me such a clear, dear, and important point: that although, of course, God is full of sympathy and care for us; and though we cannot succeed vividly to represent His sympathy otherwise than as a kind of suffering, we must not press this to mean that suffering, what we experience in our own little lives as suffering, is *as such* and *literally* in God. God is overflowing Love, *Joy*, and Delectation. I showed, I think, many and grave reasons as warnings against importing, or admitting suffering in God. I gave a detailed instance of ruin effected in a fine mind, and in all his outlook, in a man who began with that one eccentricity—real, literal suffering in God.

My Sweet: in a few days I am beginning the third and final writing of this thing; and when it is all typed and ready to go, for printing, to America—to be out in September—I shall want you to read it carefully for me, telling me if it comes home to you throughout as live and true, and if it is as clear as I can make it. I hope to have it thus ready, say, in three weeks from now.

And of course I shall greatly love seeing you here next Wednesday, 11th. As an exception, it happens that on that day the morning—say ten-thirty to twelve-thirty—would do quite well, so if afternoon would have to be shorter as to your visit, come in morning. If afternoon will really do as well, then I prefer afternoon—say four, or four-thirty, or five—for, I hope, an hour and a half.

13 VICARAGE GATE, KENSINGTON, W.8

Darling Child,   19 May, 1921.

I find I can scribble a bit this afternoon, so I will write you a letter, Dear. You gave me no coming address, so I will just send this to Friendly Green, where you may still be. At least, they will forward all right, I do not doubt.

As to the Parallel Psalter book, I had to wait, because for months I was £100 and then £150 to the *bad* at the bank; but these last weeks I have been, to

my pleased surprise, £150 to the *good*. So I could
well afford this book for you, and got it at once, with
such joy!

I well understand what you feel about religion,
suffering and caring. But please notice carefully, and
for a general principle of wise judgment, that religion,
on its human side, in so far as it is a human activity—
is subject to excesses and defects, to diseases and aber-
rations more or less special to itself, but which no
more prove anything against religion at its best—
religion as it is on God's side—than do the corresponding excesses and defects, deflections and diseases
of Art, of Science, of Politics, of Marriage, prove
aught against these kinds of life and of reality, taken
at their best and in their intendedness on God's side.
I possess a French medical psychologist's very in-
structive yet dangerously plausible, really anti-religious
book, *Les Maladies du Sentiment Religieux*. As a matter
of fact, for his mind (perhaps unbeknown to himself)
religion, the whole of religion, is these "maladies."
We live in times of such obvious transition, decline,
poverty of deep, creative conviction, of such excess of
analysis over synthesis—that it is in the air all around
us to ask questions, to poke about, to wonder, to
drift, to use the microscope; where to become and
to be, to produce reality, to adore and to will, and to
see things in the large and upon the whole, and at
their best, is what we all require.

As to religion and caring for our dear ones, I enclose
for you to keep the glorious profession of faith and of
love of St. Bernard on occasion of the death of his half-
brother and fellow-Cistercian (=strict Benedictine)
monk Gerard. The entire sermon is most touching. But

is not this bit vibratingly beautiful? I have translated
it as well as I could; but it has lost, alas, a good deal
in the process!

I shall not be sending you, Sweet, that "Suffering
and God" address, at least not typed, after all. I found
on reflection, and after getting some letters from
hearers of it, that it was little or no use to publish the
thing as it stands—that it really requires, for such as
do not already hold its views, an entire new section,
a section i. which would draw out the right principles
and proper method for such an inquiry. You see, my
Sweet, young people always just go ahead on such
points, as though they were talking, say, of Sargent's
portraits or of Drinkwater's plays, or at least of things
which we *can* hold, overlook, comprehend. But as to
God, we can, indeed, be sure, very sure, of Him—
He is implied in all our thinking, feeling, willing,
doing; it is the implicit faith in the reality and the
useful work of truth, of goodness, of life which will
never die out for long amongst mankind. And we can,
we do, gain vivid experience of Him, if only we will
die, die, day and night, to self. We can thus increasingly *apprehend* Him—can know really about Him,
the head, the source of all reality and of all sense of
reality. But we cannot encircle Him, map Him out,
exhaustively explain Him. We cannot really say, as
these objectors cheerfully argued: "If He feels joy,
He must also feel pain": we cannot, for we thus
assume that we are dealing with a fellow human
being; that by "feeling" in God we mean no other,
no more, than by "feeling" in man. Nor can we argue,
as another pressed upon me, that *he* would break his
heart, if his only son took to an impure life; how

much more then must God break His heart, if and
when any of us gravely sins. We cannot so argue,
because here again we do not encircle, penetrate God;
and because we must not press points in ways and degrees which would contradict certain other, and really
deeper, intimations and requirements of the religious
sense. Now the deepest intimation and requirement
we really have got—though sadly weakened in many
of us by the fever and rush of life since about A.D. 1790
—is Being (as distinct from Becoming), is Perfection
(as distinct from Attempting), is indeed Action, but
not Change. *Of course* change in ourselves, in the
sense of becoming better and better in all things;
but this—this need of change in us, comes simply
from our imperfection. We are not God. Yet how we
need Him! And this, then, not as just a larger ourselves, not as a larger Becoming, but as Being, as
Joy Pure and Undefiled.

Now this, with the St. Bernard which I will now copy
for you, must do for to-day, my Child.

13 VICARAGE GATE

30 May, 1921.

Am now, Child, in midst of proof correction of
my *Essays*, as well as (when these leave me a pause)
at work on the book. So I dare not write a long letter
—only something to go with the accompanying MS.
of *Suffering and God*. I am rather ashamed to lend,
even you, this still not sufficiently clarified thing.
Show it to no one else. You may, I trust, learn from
it, even so. I have had further adhesions to its main
positions.

I have been very happy over the thought of your visit to Mrs. Rice, a real short holiday. So glad peace is reigning within. How wise the *Imitation* is, in always preparing the soul for its desolate times; for if once we learn, and continue to learn better and better, how to keep on steadily during those times and to profit by them, *why* we have learnt the secret of solid advance.

Mrs. L—— has written from America. Evidently going on steadily and well. She will, I believe though, grow richer in soul and outlook.

I will have to attend D. Farquhar's address before our L.S.S.R. meeting on 7 June, about Indian Pantheism—as soon as ever his reaches me. A great scholar for the *Indian* side of the question—but strangely inferior as soon as ever he comes to treat of the Christian positions. This, though he is a devoted Christian missionary, with at least thirty years of Christian religious thinking behind him. Why is this? I am sure of the answer. Because as a Protestant Nonconformist, he looks at all the Christian side from far too individualistic, sectarian, single Bible-texts, point of view. You cannot get these great questions solved, or even only stated *greatly*—except through much history, institutions, Church appurtenances. No doubt these things will not, alone, suffice; they can even be taken in a way that stifles. Yet they *are* wanted. A child may cut itself with the table-knife, yet such a knife is necessary for cutting the bread.

Trust no headaches, Child.

Loving old,

Uncle.

13 VICARAGE GATE, KENSINGTON, W.8

Child Mine,   21 July, 1921.

I have now lots to answer, lots to tell. But first about
the books. I am sending you three books about *Socrates*
—two are presents, one is a loan; and a fourth book as
a help—an adviser—with regard to sensitiveness.

1. I want you first to read John Burnet's analysis
of the evidence as to Socrates, and *his* estimate as to
the influences which played upon Socrates's mind,
and the way in which he sorted them out and developed them. You will find this in Burnet's edition of
Plato's *Phædo* (which I lend you), pages ix-lvi. I want
you to study these pages twice through, most carefully.

2. Then take (in the volume I give you of Xenophon's *Anabàsis* and *Memorabilia*) the "Memorabilia of
Socrates," pages 349-507. This, too, I want read through
at least twice (with the notes, as far as you can follow
these; and looking up all sites in your *Classical Atlas*).
Please keep alive everywhere to Socrates's *irony*; he
hardly ever opens his mouth without it colouring what
he says; take him literally and you mostly make him
say the very opposite he means. Try, too, to trace
the influence of the Sophists, of Anaxagoras, of the
Pythagoreans and Orphics, etc.: Burnet ought to have
helped you towards this. And finally contrast his
teachings and tone with the Christians' outlook.

3. Then take the *Four Socratic Dialogues of Plato*,
translated by Jowett with Preface by Edward Caird,
which I give you.—First, a double reading of Caird's
Preface, pages v–xi. Then the Analysis of the "Eúthyphro," pages 1–9. Then the "Eúthyphro" itself, pages
10–36, twice. The same with the "Apology," the "Crito"

(*Creito*) and the *Phædo*.—Note again in these four *Dialogues*, Socrates's irony, the sources of his ideas, and their limits and peculiarities — when compared with Xenophon's account of them, and still more when compared with the Christian outlook. (Of course pre-existence is a myth, and there do not really occur any memories from such a pre-existence.)

When you have done all this, I should like you to re-read again Burnet's account, and to see how far you yourself have found it true. (You will remember that I utilised Burnet's elucidation of all that the *philosopher* Socrates owed to the *religious* (Pythagorean and Orphic), in my criticism of Corrance, and his turning from the Sun, definite religion, to the Moon, philosophy.)

4. I give you Faber's *Spiritual Conferences* because, although I do not believe him to be a truly classical spiritual writer, several of these conferences will—at least can, I think—help you much. I am thinking especially of "Kindness," 1–53; "Wounded Feelings," 260–74; "The Monotony of Piety," 314–32; and "All Men have a Special Vocation," 375–96. Surely, Sweet, there is much, much knowledge of our poor human heart here. I feel that Faber's limitations are, at bottom, three. (i.) He hardly ever leaves anything to his hearers or readers to develop further by and for themselves. He was cleverly called "the spiritual Dickens" by a man who pointed out the same peculiarity in Dickens. (ii.) He has got a touch—indeed more than a touch—of vulgarity—he can, at times, speak as though he were a Salvation Army Hallelujah lass. And (iii.) he never quite got beyond the anti-Protestantism so common amongst our converts—

devotion to the Blessed Virgin, loyalty towards the
Pope, and the like, were, because antipathetic to
Protestants, underlined by, revelled in by, Faber to
a degree which, at times, put them out of their
Catholic proportion, their Catholic perspective. He
would thus, instead of a continuator of the grand
old pre-Reformation Catholic piety of England,
become an imitation—an affectation—of Italian, of
Neapolitan piety. But you will find only little of
all this in this volume, I think. Faber sprang from an
originally French, Huguenot family; hence, in part,
I do not doubt, his love of point, paradox, hyperbole.

As to your news and questions, Dear.

There is, to my delight, once more your fundamental experience of, and call to Recollection—the
Prayer of simple Quiet. This is, of course, a true, deep
grace of God; it is by being very faithful to it, by
feeding it, by dropping what weakens or drives it
away, that you will become happy and holy. How
beautifully simple! I quite understand the two stages
of it—the stage of distractions and of having to drive
—to strive to drive them away; and then the stage of
a living, somehow self-acting recollection—with God,
His peace, power and presence, right in the midst of
this rose of spiritual fragrance.

I think you could pretty easily weaken, or delay,
this sense by too much dwelling (even from the best
of motives) upon the criticisms of yourself, such as
you mention. I do not believe in getting peace from
seeking (and even finding) that the criticism was not
deserved. And indeed even if it was entirely not
deserved, our minding criticism so very much—its
hurting us so much: this is surely a weakness, a

faulty condition, at least of our nerves. If and when we become genuinely deeply humble, we shall feel that we very certainly are full of faults, either those particular faults, or other faults—it will be too much of a most certain fact to our minds, for any possible, or even obvious mistake as to the fault—the kind of fault—to surprise or vex us out of our peace. Still, of course, even then—then especially—we would quietly and shortly look as to whether we can find the fault in us, and if we found it would ask Christ Our Lord to help us weed it out or drop it. Yet always would I expect to find you to grow more by feeding the quiet within you than by direct self-examinings or self-fightings. These two latter things also to exist in your life—but much less, less centrally than the feeding of the quiet and the loving of God, Christ, and others in it.

As to *Confession*, I have a certain complication about it in my mind, which, I expect, is not very common even amongst my own people. You see, with the Sacraments, as, indeed, with all other points of religion, I so love to trace the great lines of their development, and to find out, and to cling to, whatever may be of the essence of the Catholic doctrine and practice. Applying this to Confession I find (as you can read in full in my *Mystical Element*) that the essential, primitive, unchangeable part is *obligatory* Confession in case of *Grave Sin*. The Protestant Reformers abolished the *Obligation* in any and every instance. And now High Churchmen have come to recommend fairly frequent Confession, in imitation of our (R.C.) late mediaeval, and still more, our modern habit. Now I do not doubt that fairly frequent Confession can help on souls, yet

I love to keep quite clear in my own mind an element of *Obligation* which the Protestant Reformers unhappily lost—abolished; and an element of Conditionality—Freedom—with regard to the late mediaeval and modern Frequent Confession, which even my High Anglican friends are lacking in. I want, in this point also, a wise, firm circumspection. But to take the practice of Confession as simply in all circumstances not obligatory—as always what we call "Confession of Devotion," I quite see that also taken this way, the soul can get real help and growth in self-knowledge, humility, etc., from it. Since *our*, late centuries, discipline in the matter is just disciplinary—i.e. since Rome herself could relax it any way up to, excluding, Confessions for Grave Sin, it is certainly not for me to press you to very frequent Confessions of Devotion. I myself go every fortnight or every three weeks—but this, simply because of the extant *discipline* of the Church, and because I feel I ought not to exempt myself from it. I expect that every six months would be quite frequent enough for yourself, to get all the good, in your particular life and particular *attrait*, that the practice would be likely to give you. Of course, you would have to learn to do so with a special kind of freedom and a special kind of strictness according to the special demands of God upon your soul. *Cela varie*, Huvelin would have said, *entre âme et âme*.

I have, these last days, been seeing a former fellow-student of Gertrude's, for many years an Agnostic, then a fervent High Anglican; who, now thirty-eight, is inclining to take herself back, to look out for No. 1, to grumble and to turn sour. Am doing what I can for her: pray for her. Have explained how she requires a second conversion—this time against the dust and drear when the physical enthusiasm dwindles.

The American, Miss Branham, who went to try her call, with those strict, field-working Benedictinesses, has just written to say she is very happy as a hard-worked Postulant; I really think she will succeed: a fine instance of the genuineness of such calls.

I do wish those headaches would go. Will tell Thekla what you say for her when I see her.

13 VICARAGE GATE, W.8

My darling Gwen-Child, 27 July, 1921.

Let me now try first to explain about *Confession*. You see, the very earliest Christian position as to grave (="Mortal") sin was that a man or woman, one baptised as an adult (and thereby purified from his or her sins), did not again fall into such grave sins. Hence the question as to what he or she should do, in case they *did*, in fact, relapse, did not then arise. (You can find traces of these conditions and con-victions in *Saint John's Epistles*, and other nooks and corners of the New Testament.) But I need not tell you that only a little time was, in most regions of the nascent Church, necessary for this first intense martyr fervour to abate, and for the question concerned to become very much alive and fully practical. If you look in *Tertullian* (perhaps the selection you possess would suffice, but anyhow in others of his writings he is quite plain), you will find "the second plank after shipwreck"—the "first plank" being baptism. What *is* "the second plank"? "The second plank" is Christian

G

Penance or Penitence. Of what does this consist? It consists of three parts, *each of which in case of grave* (=mortal) *sin, is necessary for the Divine Forgiveness*: contrition, *confession*, and satisfaction. The meaning of "contrition" is, of course, quite clear; then, as now, it means a definite sorrow for having committed those sins, a sorrow from the motive of the love of God, and a deliberate, firm resolution of amendment! The meaning of "satisfaction," too, remains substantially the same—the restoration, as far as possible, of whatever we may have unjustly taken away— conjugal fidelity, or health, or fortune, etc.—but the "confession" then meant, for several centuries, a *Public* confession, in the Christian Church Assembly, before, and into the hands of, the *Bishop*. The bishop it was who, during the earlier time, only after a considerable space filled with works and proofs of penitence, solemnly, again in the Christian Church Assembly, reconciled the sinner with God—absolved him from his sins, in the name and by the power of Christ.

Now in those early centuries *there was no habit of confession for venial sins*. I suppose that now and then such a thing as private confession for venial sins happened. But if it did, it must have been rarely, since I do not know of any documents attesting such confessions. In any case, it is entirely clear that such confessions were not considered obligatory—were not believed to be essential to reconciliation with God. The proof of this is that even the strictest Roman Catholic theologians to this hour teach that we cannot press strict obligation to beyond grave (=mortal) sins; that the confession of venial sins (such as has become general in the Roman Catholic Church since, say, A.D. 1350 or a little earlier) can only be pressed on the ground of its being conceited not to follow the prevalent discipline of the Church, and on the ground of the spiritual utility, etc. In strictness, even with us Roman Catholics, a soul which has committed no grave sin—is not conscious of an unconfessed grave sin—would not be obliged to more than to present itself, once a year, at Eastertide, to the priest, to tell him it had no grave sin to confess, and to ask his blessing (even this only because of certain Decrees of Councils in about 1260 and 1560).

Now confessions for venial sin we call confessions of *Devotion*—confessions for mortal sin we call confessions of *Obligation*. My feeling I somehow *must* go to confession (for venial sin) does not make such confession into a confession of obligation; nor contrariwise, does my not feeling any obligation to confess unconfessed mortal sin make such confession into a confession of devotion. What the Church thinks, not what you or I feel or think, is here decisive and discriminative.

Now for myself, upon the whole, I regret, I will not say all confessions of devotion; I believe, on the contrary, that they have helped to train and sanctify many a soul. Also, I am glad that Anglicans should practise them—in moderation and wisely. But what I mind much more is the breach at the Reformation, by the Protestant reformers, even in England—the breach, not in the then prevalent practice of confessions of devotion, but in the immemorial doctrine and conviction of *confessions of obligation*. It was then that the conviction was abandoned that a Christian (if he

have the physical opportunity of finding a priest)
cannot attain forgiveness for mortal sin, without
confession, as one of the three essential conditions of
Christian Penitence.—True, the fathers of Anglicanism
managed, most wisely, to retain the doctrine and
practice of confession, for all souls which spontaneously
wanted it, which felt it would help them. And again
I do not doubt that many a High Churchman has in
his heart of hearts continued the old pre-Reformation,
Catholic conviction of the *necessity*, the *obligation*, of
confession *in case of grave sins*. Yet, alas, this is not the
official position—he is not free to press it—confession
remains, officially, even for grave sin—amongst Anglicans—less obligatory than, amongst Roman Catholics,
is confession for venial sin (for here, as explained, there
is the fear of going against the present discipline of
the Church, etc.).

So you can now understand, I hope, my Child, what
I meant in this whole matter. It seems to me that, for
yourself, you will do well by using confessions of
devotion in moderation and with wisdom and peace-
fulness; and that (if you can do so without strain and
mental contortion) it will be well if you can add to
this practice the conviction that, if you had grave
sin on your conscience, you would then be *bound* to
confess.—You see, this, as regards your own practice
of confession, introduces no complication of any kind.
It only somewhat complicates your *Anglican* outlook.
And, Blessing, the cry of my old heart is to be—to
become—a not all unworthy follower of Him who
broke not the bruised reed and quenched not the
burning flax!—so there, enough about *that*!

My holiday begins *certainly* on 11 August, possibly

on 8 August (i.e. if they have me at Farnham Castle from 8 August to 11 August—when I join Eva and Pucky at Thursley). I have written to the bishop proposing, as an alternative, to come to them *after* Thursley, i.e. from Friday, 9 September, to Monday, 12 September.

Am trying hard to get you a good second-hand copy of Jowett's Plato translation complete. It is in *that* that I intend to march you through certain dialogues for Plato himself, when you have done the Socrates reading.

Loving Uncle,
H.

About Harry's book—another time!

13 VICARAGE GATE, W.8

My darling Gwen,   29 July, 1921.

Thanks much for letter.

1. About confession, then, we have got all clear. I am feeling that it will be a good thing for you to go to the amount you propose, also for the reason that it still further forms you along the lines of the moderate, *Church* mystical, the mixed type—by far the safer and richer. That very balanced, wide-seeing American psychologist of religion, whom I saw in his room some days back, is full of the all-importance of the difference between Pure or Sheer or Exaggerated Mysticism (which is akin to Pantheism or some kinds of Spiritualism) and Mixed or Moderate Mysticism, which finds its completion, articulation and safety in history and institutions. The latter Mysticism both gives to, and gets from, history and institutions much, very much.

2. About the Sadhu: I enclose the memorandum
I drew up, at the request of Canon Streeter and
Mr. Appasamy, towards the construction and orien-
tation of their book on the Sadhu. I was much struck
with how far more rich and probing the outlook was
of the young Indian layman, the son of Indian converts to Christianity, than the Englishman, a cleric—
a canon of an historic Christian church, and de-
scended from a long Christian ancestry—a man
middle-aged, too. It was Appasamy who—how often
—was and is puzzled by the Sadhu's insistence upon
direct inspiration—that he does nothing except under
such. "But please, Baron, is this necessary? Cannot,
and does not God speak to us also through various
means which spring from Him?" The canon—a man
whom I like, he is so clean and so serious, and so
pacific and sweet in discussion—would never ask
such a question; indeed I doubt not that his chief
interest in the Sadhu springs from this Indian, and,
in some ways, supremely individualist, attitude. I say
"in some ways," for, after all, his mind and words
are—most fortunately for all—saturated with what he
finds in the New Testament.

I find the Sadhu to be a fine, firm character—a
devoted will, but to have curiously little mind. I think
if he had more mind (and remained as finely un-
fanatical as he now is) he could not think, say, the
following strangely unperceptive thoughts. For one
thing, he told me himself, upon my questioning him
very carefully on the point that, during the thirteen
years since he has been a Christian, he has *never*, not
even for some moments, experienced spiritual dryness,
spiritual desolation. I asked my close friend, Professor

N. Kemp Smith, the philosopher, a religious mind,
what he thought of this, and without hesitation he
judged that the Sadhu either did not really know
himself, or did not know what "spiritual desolation"
means, or did not understand either. Then, as to the
continual Direct Inspiration, I was lent one of his
addresses, typed, in which he specially insisted upon
this point; yet much the most alive thing in the whole
address was the exclamation: "He made us for Himself, and restless is our heart until it rests in Him,"
which very certainly comes from St. Augustine's
Confessions, Book I. chapter i. section 1.

3. As to Suggestion and Auto-Suggestion and
Religion, or at least Mystical Religion, you can find
in my *Mystical Element* certain positions, taken over
from M. Boutroux, which I still believe to be sound.
Also please read, and lend if and where this may be
wise, Father Walker on "The Psychology of the
Spiritual Exercises," in the *Hibbert Journal* for last
April, which I also send (pages 401–13 there).

(I also enclose the *Hibbert Journal* for this July,
because of the symposium in it on "Morals and
Religion." I *think* you have not yet seen my little
paper there, pages 605–10. Professor Chevalier, pages
610–15, I like, though it is perhaps too, as it were,
mathematically clear. But the other three papers are
very unsatisfying, I think.)

4. Dearie, I have plenty of money just now, so want
to tip you a five pounds for any little outing or what
not. Here it is—bless you! I heard from the bishop
yesterday, I am to come to them from 8 August to
11 August.

After all I had better send the two *Hibberts* in a

150 *Baron Von Hügel's*

separate parcel. You see, Dear, the all-important points as to Suggestion, Auto-Suggestion, Mono-Ideism, etc. are to remember (i.) that all such things, where real and fruitful, are means, methods, connections, etc.—instrumental; and (ii.) that they can be thus real and fruitful because there exist realities—above all The Reality—distinct from them and us. Religion, as such, makes straight for these latter things; Psychology, etc. may, and does, potter over those other, lesser things.

13 VICARAGE GATE

My Gwen-Child,   8 August, 1921.

Before starting to-day for my holiday, I write down this scheme of the study of this Jowett's *Plato* for you. It will go with the volumes—your own copy—as soon as such copy is found by my booksellers.

I divide up *Plato* into five groups and periods—and of these I want you to take the greatest dialogues in four of these groups and periods. (One of the groups is too hard for any but specialists.)

I. Socratic Dialogues. *Euthyphro—Apology. Crito. Phædo.* You have already done these.

II. Educational Dialogues.

    1. *Protagoras.*
    2. *Gorgias.*
    3. *Phædrus.*
    4. *Meno.*
    5. *Symposium.*

Omit the Critical Dialogues.

Read Comprehensive Dialogues—*Phædo* really belongs here. *The Republic. Work of old age. The Laws.*

I should like you always to study Jowett's Introduction carefully—then the Dialogues *twice*; and then the Introduction a last time.

Please specially watch, in the *Phædrus*, the *Meno*, the *Symposium* and the *Republic*, points taken over later by the Christian thinkers—especially St. Augustine.

I incline to recommend your beginning with the Socratic Dialogues again, and reading them here for the purpose, not of Socrates but of Plato—and reading these so as to keep the *Phædo* in its place according to the date of composition.

THE RED LION INN, THURSLEY, NEAR GODALMING,
SURREY

My darling Gwen-Child,　　　　23 August, 1921.

At last I am scribbling to you again, with plenty to say, but still in a drifting, lazy, tired holiday mood, hence shrinking away from much detail or precision. Let me number my subjects.

1. Before leaving home, I wrote you a letter of instructions as to the exact selection, order, method, etc., with which I should like you to read *Plato*; and this letter I left with my lady bookseller, to put into the parcel of Jowett's *Plato*—four volumes—as soon as they had received a well-preserved and not over-dear second-hand copy (the book has been out of print a long while now). You will see that I assume you to have carefully studied the Socratic Dialogues

*G

(including the *Phædo*, which really belongs to a later period of writing); that I group for you the other dialogues which I want you to study into four groups; and that I invite you to skip—for the present at least —the six very difficult and technical dialogues of the *critical* group. Even so, you have a large and splendidly rich field before you, and we will talk over together, and read certain great passages together, carefully, I hope and believe. I want you to get to think and feel Platonically on quite a number of points.

2. I left home on Monday, 8th, and stayed at Farnham Castle till after tea on the 11th. How full up, and what a *va et vient* it was, and, apparently, always is there! The widow of an Episcopalian Bishop of Glasgow and her daughter; another golden-haired young lady, and Walter Frere, an old friend of mine, head of the Community of the Resurrection at Mirfield, Yorks, there—the ladies till Wednesday morning, Frere till Thursday morning. Then on Wednesday, from eleven till six, some sixteen clerics, suffragan bishops, canons, rectors, etc., for a conference on Faith Healing. Then by tea-time on Wednesday the Fords—the parents and the seven children. And on the Thursday by lunch-time, the Episcopalian Bishop of New York and two other gentlemen for the night. Miss Winnie Talbot and the secretary, Miss Wilcox, were there all the time. . . .

4. The bishop asked me to say a few words to those assembled Faith-Healing clerics, with two of whom I got some pleasant talk before and later on. I attempted three points. That I could not feel the force of the appeal to St. Paul's account of the faith-healers in the Church of Corinth, since *there* we have the uprush of

a mass of forces and influences, strong with the strength of an immense new religion—forces and influences in no wise directly produced, or even intended, by St. Paul, but simply regulated, graduated by him, seeing that they existed in chaotic force all around him. He had not looked to see what the world then required, nor had lent an ear to what it asked for, and had then assumed the presence of these powers amongst his Christians. No: the powers were *there*, seethingly, obtrusively; because they were there, he organised and utilised them.—Did my hearers feel they possessed such powers? Were these their powers so strong as to demand regulation, graduation? If not, was it not *unreal* (surely, a great weakness in religion!) to organise, even to discuss, as though the demand for such things, or even the desirableness of such things, were equal to their supply, to their obtrusive presence?—That this my point was not controversially meant—that I should feel the same about my own people: I did not see indications of their possessing such *individual* faith-healing powers, and did not see how, unless and until they possessed them, it was *real* to discuss their utilisation.—My second point was that I felt Extreme Unction, prac- tised as it was amongst ourselves as a sacrament— officially and not as an individual gift—a rite so ancient as to be clearly taught in the New Testament, in the Epistle of St. James—to stand on quite a different plane. That I should love to see them work for the new recognition of this. Let them have the insight and the courage to part company with Luther's rejection of that Epistle, and to work for the acceptation of that touchingly beautiful, most helpful rite—the anointing

of the dangerously sick. And my third point was to
beware, in either case, of action parallel with that of
the physician, or in supplantation of him. We are
Christians, not Christian Scientists. The action of the
physician should move upwards, from the body, his
chief concern, to the mind—and with God in the background. The action of the priest should move downwards—from God as his central concern, to the human
soul and the body at last. That is, let them strive to
become, not faith-healers but saints. How I have
learnt to see that even the tenderness, the social
interest and sympathy of Christ, was so entrancing and
so operative because proceeding from, and throughout
conjoined with, a lofty sanctity, an awful holiness—
the bending of loftiness, the mercy of purity: the two
—not any one of these things—the two together—
with the Holiness, the closest union of God as the
starting and returning point of the whole Anecdote:
how the Good Shepherd nuns attain to successes with
fallen women, greater than any other body, whether
Roman Catholic or not.

5. I should love to write on, but must now go to
Puck—who has to be out of this inn. Am here till
9 September; then home. Poor Hillie has had a
sudden violent attack of influenza—been very weak,
but is mending now. Was moved to Vicarage Gate.

Loving Uncle-Father,

H.

7 October, 1921.

You bring up, my Gwen-Child, a point which
I suppose you really feel an objection. Even if you

do not feel it so, I think it well worth while to clear
out this corner of your mind, so as to make quite sure
that you correctly seize the truly great doctrine of
Purgatory. I want, then, to make sure that you
clearly understand that, according to that doctrine,
suffering (*rightly accepted* suffering) is indeed usually
necessary for, is inherent in, the purification from
sin, evil habits, etc. But it makes no substantial distinction between such purification as taking place
already here or taking place in the Beyond. In all our
Retreats we are taught that it will have been our
own fault, if the sufferings of our life here have not
sufficed to purify us from our sins and evil habits.
Of course, even very great sufferings would not,
simply of themselves, purify us from even small evil
habits. It is only suffering *meekly accepted, willed, trans-
figured by love of God, of Christ*—it is only such that will
purify or cure anything. This is so true that, where the
love is perfect, this *love alone, without any suffering* not
directly prompted by itself, completely blots out the
evil dispositions. Such a soul, even if previously a
great sinner, goes straight to Heaven upon its death.
Yet in all cases, Purgatory applies indifferently to
sufferings rightly borne in *this* life and the same similarly borne in *that* life. There is simply no such thing
as a Purgatory here followed, as though it had not
been, by a Purgatory hereafter.—On the contrary,
every pang God allows to reach us here, and which we
manage to bear a little well, does *a work not to be
repeated*. We become thus fitter and fitter for complete
union with Christ and God from the very minute of
our death.

I have written "a little well" on purpose. For to

suffer well is far more difficult than to act well (although the ordinary talk is that we have just "to grin and bear" suffering—we can do nothing to it or with it!!!). Holy suffering is the very crown of holy action. And God is no pedant: He can and does look to the substance of our suffering, and knows how to penetrate beyond our surface restlessness or murmurs. Indeed part of the grand work suffering effects in the soul doubtless springs from the way in which, when acute, it almost invariably humbles us: we can much less easily cut a fine figure in our own eyes over our sufferings, than we can over our actions when in peace and plenty.

You understand all the above completely, I trust? We will both do what gently, peaceably we can to have all our Purgatory—every drop of it—here; and then, and then, Heaven, the closest union, unfailing, with Pure Joy, with All Purity, with Christ, with God.

Loving old Uncle,

H.

13 VICARAGE GATE, W.8

My darling Gwen-Child,   12–14 November, 1921.

Here I am, at last again scribbling to you! I do not know whether you have gone back to the old rectory; but I will address this there, unless I hear, before putting this up, that you are at some other given address.

I have much to say, as to *your* points, and a good many things about my own experience.

1. . . .

2. I am delighted you have now read Plato's *Phædo*

four times. How fine, if gradually, you get to know all the Dialogues (except those six or seven very technical ones) as well as this one! Margaret Roper, Sir Thomas More's daughter, doted upon *Plato* in the Greek original; I shall be glad indeed if my own Niece-daughter comes to know *Plato*, almost as well, in the English translation.

3. . . .

4. I had three most happy, I hope useful, days at Beaconsfield. There were nine of us in all. Mr. W. B. Trevelyan, the head of the house—a second cousin of C. M. Trevelyan (who wrote on Wycliffe and Garibaldi); and his young sub-warden—both very High Anglican clerics; then Mr. Hockley, Rector of Liverpool, a tall, black-haired, manly creature; also Mr. Carey, second-in-command of the Cowley Fathers—a straight, simple man; a bishop returned, after eighteen years' work in Bloemfontein (South Africa), a year ago—a fatherly, genial man; a Mr. Platts, Vicar of St. Michael's, a High Ritual church close to Thekla's convent—zealous, straight; and finally a charming layman, Mr. Arthur Smallwood, Governor of Greenwich Hospital, about forty years old, with whom I got some very private talk. No; there was one man more: Father Denys, one of the three Anglican Benedictines who did not go over to Rome when, some fifteen years ago, the other twelve or so of the community of Caldy did so. I like this Father Denys much. I certainly think the position of a Benedictine not accepting the jurisdiction of the Pope a very strange one. But if "Charity covereth a multitude of sins," good faith is compatible with, and expresses itself in a multitude of strangely illogical positions.

And deliberate self-renunciation is everywhere dear and darling. And then this Father Denys is evidently a man of much spiritual shrewdness and extraordinarily wide reading.

They certainly gave me lots to do. Half an hour's speech at the preliminary meeting—as to the precise order and spirit of our conference; an address of one hour; and answers to questions on it, for another hour, on the Wednesday—all as to facts about God, specially useful to know in prayer; on Thursday, address of an hour, and answers for an hour—both as regards the facts about the soul, most useful to know in prayer.—And besides, I got some private talks with Mr. Platts, Father Denys and Mr. Smallwood (as already said).

My chief general impressions were, I think, three. (i.) What clean, good, straight, humble, earnest men! My Gwen, you can add them, I am sure, all eight, to the list of thoroughly clean men I tried to make out for you the other day. (ii.) How greatly, even in a sense excessively, they were under the spell of Rome —the mighty Mother. I felt it in their attitude towards myself, which was *very certainly* not only, not even chiefly, because of my individual personality, but because I was a Roman Catholic, trained in, and who could tell them about, that Mother Church. When I said just now, "excessive," I mean that I found them with little or no discrimination between what, with us, is the substance and unchangeable, and what is, again with us, the accident as the changing, or at least changeable, discipline of the Church.

And (iii.) that final question showed, I thought, that they attributed too much power to training, for they asked whether the spirit and life of an Abbé Huvelin should not be taught and trained into such Anglicans as were prepared for the clerical life, and especially those who were to have the care of souls. I answered that certainly it would be well, more and more to improve such preparation; but that I was confident such men as Huvelin would always be rare, anywhere and at all times. That he himself, e.g. had derived only a fragment of what he was and became, from his technical, seminary training; that I thought it would be well to teach the *average* Church student that there were—there existed—deep, rare souls, both amongst the laity and amongst the clerics, and to encourage such student to refer such rare lay-folk to the one or two deeply spiritual clerics he might be taught to know about. That if Anglicans managed to have, say, two such deeply spiritual clerics in each diocese, they should be esteemed richly favoured. That only great graces, many natural gifts, much suffering, and devoted heroism—all this or much of all this combined—would ever produce an Abbé Huvelin or a Curé d'Ars.

5. Have had a bad night, so must stop this my second go at this letter. May all be going well, or at least better with you, Child.

Loving old Father-Uncle,

H.

Poor Muriel! But how brave she is being.

2. As to Socrates (=Plato) in the (*Protagoras*), you must not apologise for your dissatisfaction on those

two points; for you are *right*, deeply right, about them.
Indeed there is also a third point, about which Socrates
(=Plato) here is equally mistaken or undiscriminative.
Let me write the three points out clearly.

(i.) Courage=knowledge; indeed virtue of any kind
=knowledge. This is certainly false, for the reasons
you give. But you will have noticed that Socrates fully
confesses that mankind at large does not take this
view. Well—mankind at large was and is, on this
point, closer to the facts, than Socrates or Plato. But,
besides men generally, there were also ancient Græco-
Roman thinkers and poets who felt and who taught
the opposite—Ovid wrote:

> Video meliora proboque;
> Deteriora sequor?

I see the better and I approve it; and (yet) I follow
the worse. Yet it is Christianity, in the completion of
the Hebrew prophetic religion, which, as against the
Græco-Roman world generally, has established the
full facts—has made me see and feel most vividly the
difference between knowledge and virtue, between a
clear head and a clean heart. On this point Kant is
deeply Christian, when he insists upon the good will
as supremely precious, and when, in his doctrine of
Radical Evil, he holds that men can and do deliberately
prefer evil to good.

(ii.) Socrates (=Plato) lumps, in his doctrine of
opposites, two very different things hopelessly together.
There is (*a*) the *contrary*, the different—say, blue and
yellow, compared with red, among colours; or notes
A, C, compared with D, among sounds. Here, two
things, say two virtues, though distinct and different

from each other, can yet, perfectly well, co-exist alongside of, or in union with, or fusion each with the other.

And there is (*b*) the *contradictory*, where one thing is the direct negation of the other; so with light, and absence of all light, etc. Here no one thing can, in any one and the same respect, contain, or be composed of, such contradictories. Thus, among the virtues, a man cannot, in precisely the same respect, be both courageous and cowardly.

(iii.) Socrates (=Plato) insists here on the good as just simply the pleasant; nor will he allow any action to be measured as to the morality except according as, at least eventually, it issues in pleasure or at least a surplusage of pleasure. Now here Socrates (=Plato) has not arrived at the profoundly important distinction between pleasure and beatitude (joy). He as yet does not see that evil doing, in certainly the greater number of cases, occurs simply because it is connected with some immediate pleasure; whereas, doing right is very frequently connected with the sacrifice of some immediate pleasure or the facing of some immediate pain—yet the yielding to sheer pleasure is the sure road to losing all beatitude, to losing even the sense of what it means. Whereas the resisting of sheer pleasure, according as right reason and duty may demand, is the sure road to joy.—I take it that Socrates (=Plato) not seeing this (iii.) is the chief cause why he holds his (1). For if once we vividly perceive that virtue consists essentially in holding out against sheer pleasure for solid joy, and that evil doing consists essentially in yielding to sheer pleasure and thus losing solid joy;

there is no need, there is no room, for knowledge, still less for the identity of knowledge with virtue. Yet note, Child, how these three errors are not errors pure and simple; but that they are stages on the way to precious truths. For: as to (1), it is true that there exists much *material* (=non-formal) evil doing; that men do what in itself is evil, often out of sheer ignorance that it *is* evil. And with his searching about for a knowledge as somehow close to virtue, Socrates (=Plato) is working his way towards a system of *objective* ethics—what, especially nowadays, we want again very badly.—As to (2), it is true that the several virtues have ultimately to be conceded as expressions, dispositions, effects, etc., of one and the same soul. Hence that, however different they may look, they must not be conceived as utterly unlike each other.— And as to (3), the end, the final measure, of virtue is indeed a state of soul the very opposite of unhappiness, constraint, disgust. Socrates (=Plato) is here after the supreme good, the utter joy, which, so far, he understates horribly by the petty term of pleasure.

So glad of your post card too, and that you have got to the *Gorgias*. You see that list I gave you will, if followed out, give you Plato *as he grows*, as he corrects himself. You will end by taking the mature Plato and correcting the immature Plato by the mature Plato, only that, no doubt, certain characteristically Hellenic weaknesses remain, more or less, to the end. E.g. of the above three points, No. (1) remains, in parts, to the very end; but not so No. (2) nor No. (3).

Loving old,
Uncle-Father.

My darling Gwen-Child,   9 December, 1921.

I have indeed been silent a long time—with, now, three dear and interesting letters of yours to answer. The reasons of this have been two. I have been a good deal tried by that arterial pressure at night; and as the doctor had told me that the less exertion there was in my day, the less I should suffer from it at night, I determined to try what cutting down everything at all avoidable would do. I am certainly now free from that pressure, or, at least, from those effects—though, I suspect, only for a little spell. Yet I am deeply thankful for it, since it means capacity for my composition work. My second reason was that I was trying to get you the *Curé d'Ars*, and that stupid postal losses—of the first order—have delayed my receiving the books till to-day. I now send you, as presents, the *Life of the Curé*, two volumes, and his *Spirit*, in one little volume. (The *Esprit* repeats in part the sayings registered in the *Vie*; but adds many fresh sayings.) I wanted to send you these volumes ready bound, but received them thus; and I think it better not first to get them bound, as you would then not have the books till after Christmas. I have cut the books open for you, as I believe myself to be expert at this. I trust and believe that the Curé's spirit will sink into your heart, and help you greatly on to geniality, humility, peace and happiness in God and for Him.

.   .   .   .   .   .

As to the young ex-curate, now one of our people: how difficult, indeed how impossible, it is to judge

whether such extreme renunciation is quite sound in
and for that particular soul, and will help it on to
deep but quite balanced self-renunciation (as in Abbé
Huvelin, the Curé d'Ars, etc.), or whether it is going
to lead to dangerous reactions, etc. The Christian
life, at its deepest and highest, is certainly not mere,
not sheer, common sense. And yet—*in the long run*—
some common sense has got to get into it, unless it
is to come to grief—something like with visions and
the excellent advice Edward Talbot gave you concerning them. There, too, one has just simply to wait,
and, meanwhile, not to treat such things as central
or as the measure of our advance or closeness to God.

As to whether converts to Rome are proselytisers.
I think *at first, as a rule*, they are. Surely this is not
difficult to understand. Such souls have generally
come, with considerable sacrifices, and, at the time,
with much spiritual light and fervour, to see and
feel sure of various facts which they before saw
fitfully or hardly at all. They very easily—all but
inevitably—forget or overlook the not inconsiderable
lights or helps they had before; and they have not
yet been long enough in the old Church to have
experienced its human poornesses nor to have themselves, within that Church, passed through desolation
and reaction. My brother told me of an interesting
conversation he had with our Bishop Brownlow, after
the latter had been one of our priests and then a
bishop some forty-eight years since he had been an
Anglican High Church curate. My brother told him
how he sometimes felt himself to be possibly quite
wrong in not being more active and enterprising in
trying to gain individual Protestants to the Church.

That, as a matter of fact, he did nothing direct in this way—he never took the first step. The bishop answered that, after the first few years of his Roman Catholic life, when his zeal was restless and, he had now long thought, indiscreet, he also had never pressed anyone; had never taken the first step with anyone; that he had now seen for many a long year how easy it is to disturb souls from out of what contains much truth and which they *can* and *do* assimilate to their spiritual profit, and to push and strain them up to something to which they are not really called and of which they do not know what to make. That his conscience did not upbraid him in this matter for the many later years of his priestly and episcopal life; and that as to those first years he hoped that he had not been as unwise as he might have been.

Also, an experienced old priest (himself an early convert to the Roman Catholic Church) once told me that he had long found it a bad sign when *converts* were not at least inclined to be active proselytisers. That with *born* Roman Catholics it was different: these could be thoroughly zealous in their religion, and yet not be thus active, or inclined to be thus active.

As to myself, I find myself inclined to be very zealous to help souls to make the most of what they already have; and, if they come to think of moving, to test them to the uttermost. And again, to do all I can to make the old Church as inhabitable *intellectually* as ever I can—not because the intellect is the most important thing in religion—it is not; but because the old Church already possesses in full the knowledge and the aids to *spirituality*, whilst, for various reasons which would fill a volume, it is much less strong as regards

the needs, rights and duties of the mental life. This
my second zeal includes the ardent wish and hope of
serving sore and sulky, fallen-off or falling-off Roman
Catholics—to heal their wounds and bring them back.
One fallen-away Roman Catholic gives me more pain
than a *hundred* accessions to the Church give me joy.
For it is the *sticking it* which really matters in these
things and which is difficult.

As to *Mother Julian*, where on earth has my Gwen-
child acquired the notion that she was an Anglican!
An Anglican in A.D. 1360? My Gwen, we must do
some Church history later on! Of course she accepted
the Pope as she accepted Christ and as she accepted
God; although there was then no occasion to put
this forward.

What you say about prayer, Sweet, is all very true,
very solid. I know well what you mean. But though
we will most rightly shrink from saying that this or
that in it is God: yet it is God, His Reality, His Distinctness from yet great Closeness to us, it is this grand
Over-againstness which through, and in, and on occasion of what you describe we experience in our little
degree. What comes last in our analysis of such states,
is first in real existence. I enclose for you a little article
which (as all except my big book) was spontaneously
asked of me, title included. Do not, Dear, dwell much
upon or worry about the Pope. It is not for *that* that
I send it to you. Nor do I want you to lend it for *that*
to others who might be pressed or worried by it. I send
it because of the *contrata* bit; and because I am utterly
sure that this is the direct antidote to the all but
universal Pantheism of our times. Before people worry
about the Church or even about Christ, they must be

helped to get God—their notions as to God—sound and strong.

I also include a fine letter of Mrs. Clement Webb, because you will admire what she says about suffering, and because of the charming bit about Richard and yourself. I do not require it back.

As to the Sadhu, I feel with you that we ought never to forget his non-Europeanness. How strange that *profound* difference between East and West. Why, in some real way, the Sadhu, all Christian though he be, is further away than are Plato and even Socrates! The Sadhu's visions are strangely wooden, *leathery* things, astonishingly other than, and inferior to, the revelations or visions of Mother Julian or of St. Teresa. It is in this matter especially that the object of the book—its object in the mind of Streeter, not, I think, of Appasamy—is not attained: the object being to show that a man as entirely outside of any Christian body or Church, can be as deep and delicate, as valuable a mystic, as are the mystics belonging to the Church. Streeter really proves the opposite of what he wants to prove.

As to Plato, I am delighted you are taking to him so strongly. I hope you will end by being steeped in him; by having read all the Dialogues we have fixed upon at least four times each; and that you will come to be able to compare Dialogue with Dialogue, and to use Plato generally, for comparison and criticism in your non-Platonic reading. I am trying to follow you in these your Plato readings: have so done the *Protagoras* and half of the *Gorgias*. So glad you are at the *Phædrus* and soon at the *Symposium*. And mind to admire the *Meno*—I love it!

As to taking the three children abroad for those
three months, how excellent! Yet there is one modi-
fication of your plan which (but for possible valid
reasons contrary, unknown to me) would seem an
improvement to me. You very rightly regret the lack
of German and Italian among you four. But why not
hold out Germany and Italy as a reward, some other
year, of German and Italian acquired at least by
some of you? You would this coming 1922 go to *France*
and, if you liked, *French* Switzerland, staying, say, a
week or ten days in Paris—there seeing thoroughly
the great galleries, Versailles, Fontainebleau, etc. Then
to the great cathedral cities—Rouen, Tours, Orleans,
etc., and staying quietly, for, say, a month, in Brittany,
there really to know that fine earnest race. I am very
sure that staying in new countries, amongst other races,
is an immensely educative influence. But you must
really stay with them, speaking their language, sharing
their life. And I am equally sure that mere *travel*,
mere maximum moving about, is sterilising rather
than improving.

Loving old Uncle-Father,

H.

13 VICARAGE GATE, W.8

13 December, 1921.

So glad you have got the books, and letters—and
article packet. No hurry for a letter from you, though
it will be most welcome when it comes!

This is merely to express my distress that you should
have attempted Plato's *Parmenides* or the *Philebus*. Have

you forgotten how we settled that you would not touch
any of the six Critical Dialogues, as all being far too
difficult? I think that resolution most important, as
otherwise you will get bewildered, strained, and then
sick of Plato. You have plenty of him to read: *Meno*,
Cratylus, the *Republic*—as long as four or five ordinary
Dialogues—and the *Laws*, even longer; and then all
over again and again, comparing one with the others.

As to the Curé d'Ars pray read the two big volumes
before the little one. You will see how sweet old
Mlle. Ars is also.

F. v. H.

13 VICARAGE GATE, LONDON, W.8

20 January, 1922.

Here I am, my darling Gwen-Child, scribbling to
you after getting released, only last night at eleven-
thirty (when I could turn into bed), from my last
three weeks' grind. I wonder a little, sometimes, my
little old thing, whether you quite realise the costingness of my life—what a lot it necessarily takes out of
me, how little of nerve and brain force it leaves me,
when my direct work of thinking and exploring in
and with Faith, Love and Practice has been done?
You see I cannot apprehend anything seriously without tension, I mean my very way of taking anything
involves much tension. And this is why there readily
come misgivings to me when I gain any great influence
either with young men or with women (whether young
or not). For both these sets of God's creatures—of my
fellow-creatures—cannot, I think, stand much tension.

They either break down physically under it, or their faith collapses under the strain, or (the best that can happen to them) they either get away from such strongly *tensional* individuals, or learn to dwell in such individuals, upon the harmonies in them and not the tensions—anyhow, my Dearie, the costliness, at least to myself, of the kind of work I have again been at, *plus* the *endless* business, friendliness, etc., of the time of year, have alone caused my silence.

I find that I have *four* letters from you unanswered, except by a post card for the first, and another post card for the last one. I will first write some words about each of your chief points and, indeed, about yourself generally. And I will then tell the chief doings and experiencings since last I wrote you a letter.

First as to the letter 13 December. I am so glad that you then, and later on again, liked the Curé d'Ars so much. It seems to me you could, with great profit, absorb into your life pretty well the whole of him—in his darling simplicity, his continuous self-oblivion, his absorption in God, and yet his amazingly large attention to others, especially to the poor and the lost. I have just now been again using him amongst my illustrations, and as always, with the greatest confidence and consolation. You know that at Thekla's convent the very experienced prioress has placed a statuette (a beautiful one) of the curé in prayer on to the table in the centre of their chapter house, as an encouragement to them to persevere in their—in his— in their joint kind of prayer—of pure love.

Then I am so glad you love Plato's *Meno* so; it is one of my favourite dialogues—perhaps the one which I carry most constantly in my head.

Then there is the strange but very dear old clergyman
(here are his, somehow very sweet, letters back, with
thanks). I am very glad he has got you to read Scott's
Heart of Midlothian—a book I know well and admire
much. I am a bit surprised you had never read it!
But have you already noted one thing, Sweet? That
dear old cleric—I feel quite sure—is one more living
refutation of the "all men have something to hide"
doctrine. There is *that* about him which cannot coexist
with any sex impurity. Either he has never lost his
baptismal innocence (the more likely alternative,
I think), or he has long and long ago fully, deeply
repented of any early lapses that may have occurred.
St. Augustine is there to prove to all men of good
faith that such recovery is fully possible.

In this same letter you dwell upon how one helpful,
spiritual writer after the other turns out to be a
Roman Catholic, whereas the Protestant bodies, even
Anglicanism, have, most at least, to go to those others
for spiritual classics. I think this is no prejudice of
yours, my Gwen-child. But I think a *certain* advantage
is extant on the other side. Not, I think, in Protestantism
as such even there; but because, alongside of much
licence, Protestantism has at least ended by leaving
liberty to scholars. I mean even such liberty as is
necessary for a really cogent defence of the Catholic
Faith. The official representatives of the Catholic
Church, on the contrary, have mostly, or generally,
struck away from such liberty. Yet this advantage of
Protestantism is immediately lost by it when it becomes
pointedly, polemically Protestant; it is then at once
more narrow and unseeing than is the narrowest
Roman Catholicism. And certainly the finest Roman

Catholic scholars, when and where they are allowed
elbow-room, remain the worthy descendants of those
Roman Catholic scholars who—so Mabillon the
Benedictine, Richard Simon the Oratorian, and Denys
Petau the Jesuit, all in the seventeenth century—were
respectively the founders of the science of history,
of Biblical criticism, and of the history of Christian
dogma.

As to the letter of 21 December. You understand,
of course, that I have excluded that group of Plato's
Dialogues from your reading, only because of their
great technicality and difficulty. If the day comes
when, having read and re-read all the others, you
feel you know them so well that you could understand
fresh problems raised by him upon the conclusions
reached by him so far, you could *then* try your hand
at these dialogues also. Fortunately these dialogues
are much the least beautiful in form, and contain
least of sayings directly utilisable for religion or ethics.
But they are free from any such blemishes as appear
in the *Symposium* and the *Republic*.

I shall love your getting back to Plato.

Perhaps, by now, you have seen that review of my
book in the *Times Literary Supplement*, and my letter
there in answer to it. Mr. Bruce Richmond has written
me the kindest letter about it all—that he had wished
to give me pleasure, and was so sorry he had failed.
But he added what took all distress about the incident
out of my mind—that the review was not, as I thought,
by Canon Barnes (one of the canons of Westminster
Abbey), who, in a review of a book by Dean Inge,
had written a *most* handsome sentence about my
writings, and who (I sadly thought) had now changed

his mind about my work. I still believe that my letter
was more or less necessary; but I see, as a friend
points out, that I have missed one of the chief difficulties in cases such as that of Anthony Trollope—
that he, Anthony Trollope, was, highly probably,
baptised, and validly baptised. Yet baptism, according
to the universal orthodox doctrine, implants in the
baptised soul the seeds of the supernatural life.

If I wrote the letter now, I would still bring up the
Anthony Trollopes of the world, but would declare
that I had never yet found a fully satisfactory answer
to the problem presented by such baptised persons, even
though I continued to feel that a doctrine, equivalent to
the ancient doctrine of *Limbo*, could be fruitfully used in
face of the problem of the apparently purely *natural*
goodness of at least many of the unbaptised.

And then the pathetic bit about your gardener's
father so ill; and the gardener's wife your only usual
companion at Holy Communion!

Then your letter of 29 December showed so well
how much and how exactly rightly you feel about
Christmas—that immensely warm and expansive,
lowly and homely, utterly touching feast. And I love
to think of David at Holy Communion with you
there, and then you and Olivia at a service in the
cathedral.—And then came the funeral of your
gardener's father.

What you say of the ignorance of the poor about
Our Lord and their practical heathenism is sad indeed,
yet I believe it true.

As to the young convert living out in the fields, I too
wonder about him. I mean, that he is being straight
and devoted is plain enough. But is he being *wise*?

And has he anyone wise to advise him, and does he attend to such an one?

First, off and on during December I had a good deal to do to help a lady whom I have known for, I think, fifteen years at least, a woman who has much religious influence with many souls; and who, if she succeeds in becoming more harmonious and more deep in herself, will do much pure good instead of as now, I think, not a little harm mixed with some good. She asked me to help her in all her spiritual views, practices, etc. First she wrote me out—very humbly and simply —as to where she stood, etc. I drew up, in response, a rough set of rules and proposals which she came here for me to develop to her. She was then asked to let me have a second report as to how the proposals struck her for direct execution in her life. And the second report she then furnished was carefully criticised by me in my final advice to her, which grew into a bulky affair. It was impossible to be much shorter with a person who has read very much and thought very much; who began as a Pantheistically-inclined Agnostic; and who, although she now, I am happy to say, goes to Anglican Holy Communion, and indeed also to Mass, and even to Benediction at the Carmelites here, never, I found, prays to Our Lord; indeed she declared that she never could do so!—She has undertaken to carry out, in great simplicity, the proposals which I ended by making very definite. She would strive gently to bring consistency into her life, by at least *thinking of* Our Lord at Holy Communion; and she would give as much time to visiting, and to attending to, the poor, as ever she could without neglecting other duties. She has settled now to give two afternoons

a week to them; and to try and learn by their needs—
the need of religion of a definitely historical kind—
the need of Our Lord, His Life, His Death, His Sacred
Person. She is to report at midsummer how things have
gone. My Gwen; you who have the great grace to love
and to worship Christ our Lord, pray for this soul,
please. I promise to tell you how she gets on. But,
purposely, I am not going to see her in between-whiles.

Then I have had vividly brought home to me a
difficulty (a purely social, educational difficulty which
all my life has dogged my steps)—as to what degree of
experience, learning, tension, etc., is good and wise
for such and such young people, or (even generally)
for people generally. You see, I had felt so glad and
proud at the thought of Professor Troeltsch coming
with me, next July, to Swanwick, where he would
address some seven hundred young men and young
women university students on religion. I felt so sure
that the Christian Student Movement authorities
would accept this, that I told Troeltsch of my efforts,
adding that the thing could be quite sure only after
the Executive Committee had decided in September.
But when, at end of November, I still had received
no news, I wrote to the Secretary, Christian Student
Movement, asking what had become of the plan, and
Mr. Tatlow answered that as soon as he had put the
plan to the Executive Committee (all university
students), the large majority at once protested hotly
against it. That the Christian Student Movement
Statutes opened out with a declaration that only
Christians who accept the historic Creeds could belong
to the movement; that surely also only such Christians
could be asked by the Committee to speak to the young

H

people at this, their supremely *religious*, gathering; and
that if once they let in Professor Troeltsch, they would
not be able to exclude from their platforms Quakers
or Unitarians or Theosophists. That my own case
was distinctly different—that they would much like
to have *me*; but, as to Troeltsch, no. Mr. Tatlow added
that a small minority did want to have him; and that
he had thought the matter so important, that he was
asking a certain number of experienced mature friends
of the movement what they would have him do. And
that, meanwhile, he would like me to tell him clearly
why I had thought of Troeltsch for them, and again
how I felt, now that I had their statutes and this
opposition so plainly before me. To this I answered
that I had been close friends and the most careful
student with and of Troeltsch for some thirty-five
years; that, all that time, I had learnt nothing but
good, and the rarest good, from him, since he had
helped me greatly to keep and to increase a joyous
faith in God, and had brought me back to a full (and
fuller than ever) admiration of the Golden Middle
Age. That a Quaker, several liberal Lutherans (like
Troeltsch), and a Unitarian had much helped me
religiously, I mean right up to the consolidation of
my historic, Roman Catholic, Christian faith. Hence
I had felt these young people might greatly profit,
and would hardly suffer damage from Troeltsch.—
That the mere fact of their statutes did not arrest me,
since even the best rules (and these seemed very good)
were liable to exceptions. And that I continued to
feel it very difficult to believe that even people so
young as his should not be exposed to influence far
more dangerous than could be the influence of Troeltsch

in his least orthodox strain. Besides, that Troeltsch had
spontaneously undertaken not to speak a word which
had not previously been considered by me. And yet
that his, Mr. Tatlow's, communication *had* pulled me
up in this wise, that I had been made to remember
that I was at least thirty-five when Troeltsch first
came into my life, and a fully formed man, whereas
these young people were all between eighteen and
twenty-four. And then I had had to recognise how
I had, more than once (and once to a saddening
degree), myself presupposed too much maturity, too
much carrying power in those I had influenced, and
this had had, for long, very sad results. So that, unless
the seniors he had referred the matter to were prac-
tically all *for* Troeltsch, I wanted him, Mr. Tatlow,
to decide against asking him to Swanwick. End of
December, Mr. Tatlow wrote, definitely declining
to have Professor Troeltsch at Swanwick; that I still
did not realise what immature, unformed, callow,
ignorant minds they had to deal with. But that the
officials—the mature and paid men—of the movement
would esteem it an honour to listen to Troeltsch next
September, at their London meeting. I have still to
write to Troeltsch that the Swanwick thing is off, and
that I do not think the London thing would be worth
his coming all that way. I shrink from doing so, as
it may a bit pain that very sensitive man; but I must
just do it, as well as I can!

And then, lastly, these last three weeks have been
chock full of "Priest and Prophet."

I ended by scribbling out in pencil a MS. so long
that, though I spoke for seventy minutes, I could
only use up a little over a third of the whole. I learnt

a lot in working it out. I think the chief points which
I got to see more clearly than ever before were that
Jesus was in conflict, roughly speaking, not with the
priests—*that* came only quite at the end, but with the
Pharisees, who were all *laymen to a man*; and again that
the reason of Our Lord's vehemence against them
was because, claiming to be the religious teachers of
the people at large, they made religion unbearably
heavy and complicated for *the poor*—the poor being
precisely those to whom He had come to preach the
Good Tidings. This preaching to the poor, He had
placed as the culminating work and credential of His
life, in His great answer to the inquiry of John the
Baptist; and hence the glorious "Come unto Me,"
and the "laden and heavy burdened," with *His*
contrasting "yoke" which is "sweet," and *His* burden
which is light, aims, in the first instance, at the
Pharisees. Now the descendants of the Pharisees are,
quite plainly, not (at least not necessarily) priests,
but such over-cultivated Puritan lay theologians as,
e.g. the Unitarians. They, too, have no Gospel for the
poor, whereas Jesus has, and first of all for *them*; you
and I come afterwards!—Also, the priests still, in
Jesus's time, stood for friendly contacts with matter;
the Pharisees, for vigilant hostility to all such contacts.
True, the Pharisees practised endless washings; but
these were for purification from all sorts of contacts
with matter of all kinds. And true, also, the priests
practised ablutions; yes, but they practised them as
preparations for contact with other kinds of matter,
in the sacrifice, the anointings, incense, etc. Jesus
stands out quite plainly on the contacts side: so in
the cure of the woman with the issue of blood, of the

lepers, etc. All these things were an abomination to
the Pharisees.

Well now, Sweet, good night! Oh, may you succeed
in not over-straining your precious health and in
managing some grand rest, expansion and peace.

God bless you. Pray for me.

Loving old,

Uncle-Father.

13 VICARAGE GATE, LONDON, W.8

Darling Child,   24 January, 1922.

This only in answer to the confession questions.

1. You have hit upon the very difficulty which
I foresaw for you in any at all frequent confession.
It is one which you would feel, far more definitely,
if you were a Roman Catholic, having to confess
(if a frequent communicant) at least every three
weeks, as I do.

2. Confession is for sins, and nothing else. Hence
no confession of general unworthiness, also no confession of general imperfections of your natural
character—that you are too sensitive, too vehement,
etc.: all quite true, but no more for confession than
that your nose is too long. St. François de Sales was a
good while in getting St. Chantale out of the way of
confessing such constitutional defects.

3. Give yourself not more than fifteen minutes *at
most* of quiet, leisurely, circumspect, warm and loving
preparation—gently recalling the situations in which
you have been since last confession: all this after, of
course, asking Our Lord to give you light and love

for seeing. If anything then pricks you—keep that for your confession, always confessing first whatever may be most difficult to confess, then make a gentle, quiet firm, but *not straining*, act of contrition. And after all this *no deliberate recurrence to the subject*.

4. If nothing thus pricks you—no strain, no trouble, no occupation with this fact. But, if you do go to confession notwithstanding, simply explain that you could find nothing committed since the last confession, so and so long ago; and re-confess the biggest thing you confessed before—but very gently, with your soul turned to Christ, your light and love and life.

5. If Edward Talbot recommends you to go to confession thus often (every six months) I should like you to go, otherwise, to spread out the time even more. For, as you know, in the Church's early centuries, the faithful (saintly souls included) went only for grave sin, in public confession, to the bishop. We must not expect, I do not want *that* back. Still, the relation between more or less deliberate *sin* and confession it is certainly wise to keep up, as far as possible, and not to let one's confessions degenerate into a sort of flea-hunt, a straining to discover sins.

Pray for me.

Loving old Uncle,

F. v. H.

13 VICARAGE GATE, W.8

My darling Gwen-Child,   28 February, 1922.

I *was* sorry to see your half-sheet to Aunt Mary this morning—I mean, as to your chill and sickness. For, as to your coming here for those nights, it is, of course, delicious. We *both* like this, very much. And we will have, I trust, at least two talks, won't we? I can easily manage such in the afternoons. Friday and Saturday, I have teaching; but even then we would arrange— or for after dinner—though, no, *that* is Aunt Mary's time with you.

Aunt Mary thinks you will have caught this chill in this my study, which is, of course, a further reason for distress. But I undertake to have a good fire alight half an hour before you turn up in here, unless the weather is truly summery.

I trust, though, you will now be quickly right again. You said nothing about headaches; I trust that means they have hardly molested you lately.

After our talk I had some scruples—I felt that I had, somehow, been straining your brain, and *that* for matters more of general *religiosity* than of the definite religion we love. I will try to do better next time.—Also I never asked after the children—their health; whilst you asked so nicely after us three.

Well, I also write because I like to be in touch with you on starting Lent to-morrow. I am again cutting myself off from buying any books for myself till after Easter. But *that* would hardly do for you, you buy, doubtless, so few, Sweet. You have so many trials sent you by God, Dearie—your headaches, housework (when considerable), money anxieties and bigger trials still, that I suspect the trying to meet and utilise all this extra well during the forty days will be all, and quite enough, for you, unless Edward Talbot has made some suggestions—they would be sure to be wise.

I have been having a strange correspondence with
Loisy, on a point which shows how strangely unalive
he is to the most obvious evidences counter to his
utterly inadequate *Religion of Humanity*. He actually
claims that M. Littré's last months—that all that
M. Huvelin observed then, is a fine illustration of this,
Loisy's, present conception of religion. Whereas, of
course, it is precisely the opposite. M. Littré had
lived fifty years a believer in, and propagator of, that
"Religion." And then God sent him an experience
which made him feel a new world in process of reveal-
ing itself to him, in which a keen sense of sin, a deep
contrition, were central. Loisy argues that because
M. Littré did not die an explicit Catholic or Christian,
or even Theist, there was no change within the
"Religion of Humanity." Strange obtuseness in one
usually so even excessively awake!

Well, Sweet, get well, Blessing; don't overwork either
body or mind or soul. God loves you and touches you
to love Him. What more do we want?

Loving old Fatherly,

F. v. H.

You must not hurry on the readings, all can wait!

At Holy Communion for you to-morrow morning,
Child.

13 VICARAGE GATE, W.8

My darling Gwen-Child,   11 April, 1922.

I want you to get a letter from me on the day of
Olivia's confirmation. Indeed I have also written
herself a little one—enclosed—which pray give to her.

I so love to trust and believe that she will take the act really seriously, and that the Christian's fight against "self"—whatever may be the particular form and degree of "self" in the particular soul—will begin, or rather will grow deeper and firmer, with her to-morrow.

My darling Niece-Child! *How* happy I am to think of you in bed, and in bed, and in bed, and not doing *anything*, not even reading, beyond just what your strength permits! What a lot we can grow spiritually— that is, how much more solidly anchored in the peace and beatitude of God we can become—by simply thus resigning ourselves, as cheerfully as possible, to such do-nothing, which indeed, where and when nature requires it, can be most refreshing.

I am so glad, too, you listen and watch the birds. I shall try and get for you a "remainder" copy (the book is quite out of print) of Alfred Newton's *Dictionary of Birds*—a truly engrossing work. There you can read up all about the particular habits, migrations, etc., of each of these birds.

I have striven to find for you those L.S.S.R. remarks of mine on the four papers about God—so far without success. But I do not doubt I shall end by finding and sending you them. The two Beaconsfield addresses are, I find, in a lady's hands, who has promised their early return. These also you shall have as soon as I get them back, but to-day I send you something that I spoke a week ago at an extra meeting of our L.S.S.R. The copy of my remarks is for you to keep; the abstract of Mr. Joseph Wicksteed's paper is for you to return some time, when quite done with. Joseph Wicksteed is the son of that very noble man—certainly a most

*H

striking intelligence — Philip Wicksteed (great on Dante and Aquinas).

I was very happy, though, whilst working at this criticism of mine; my toil at my new book helped me greatly there.

I loved both your little letters, dear Child; but never write when feeling too tired—you shall have a copy, all your own, of Charles Foucauld; but just at this moment I have lent *this* copy, which I wanted to return to you at once, to a man friend. I felt that Foucauld's heroic life would draw him, somehow, out of his deep depression.

Have you thought of Scott's Waverley Novels for reading, when you want to read and yet are too tired for harder books? I think you do not know them— certainly not all; the *Heart of Midlothian* was new to you—you would find *The Antiquary, Old Mortality, Rob Roy, Quentin Durward, Kenilworth, Fortunes of Nigel, Peveril of the Peak*, first rate. But I will not press you, because I myself, when very tired, find but little help in novels; to lie in the dark room or to prowl in the open with Puck—that does me far more good!

We shall love to have you for that night; and if you could turn up by five or even six, you and I might have a good talk before dinner—I shall keep myself free for *that*; after dinner I shall want Aunt Mary to have you.—I will show you that big history of De Rancé and the beginnings of the Trappists, because I fancy it would much interest you; as sometimes a long detailed book is better for browsing through, when one is ill, than are shorter, more concentrated affairs.

Darling Puck has a cyst on the right side of his neck—was with the vet. yesterday—but this very experienced man says that we can enjoy the darling little friend still for several years.

How stupid of me to think you could walk about, and stand, etc., amongst your poor! But London shopping—that, too, is surely not the thing for you!

Limit it and the like, Dear, all you can, pray!

Loving old Uncle,

F. v. H.

On Maundy Thursday, day after to-morrow, at my Holy Communion, on that, one of my dearest days, the little old Niece-Child will, of course, be very specially prayed for, and Olivia, indeed all three, and H—— too! God bless you, Child.

13 VICARAGE GATE, KENSINGTON

From Letter of 23 May, 1922.

I am most glad you specially love the Psalms for vocal prayer—you are here, as I find so generally with you, entirely in the mind of the Church. But I trust that you do not neglect the Our Father, the Apostles' Creed, and the Acts of Faith, Hope and Charity and Contrition—the first and these last in all your morning and night prayers.—My business began with that meeting of our L.S.S.R. in this house, when I tried to show that Our Lord's vehemence against the Pharisees was indeed sincere, and must be taken by us as indicating grave error in the Pharisees, yet that it also was a revival, after some six hundred years, of the old, pre-exilic tone and form of prophetic denunciation. Amos, Hosea, Isaiah,

Jeremiah, they all, pretty well unbrokenly, speak as
though the only sinners on the land were the men who
went to church!—as though only a quite perfect moral
life (an ideal never quite attained) left public worship
anything but a thing without value to God or man—
indeed a thing abominable to God and His prophets.
There is quite demonstrably here a certain exaggera-
tion, an "either . . . or," instead of "both . . . and."
History teaches us quite plainly that there exists no
such thing as strong and persistent religion without
public worship, and no public worship which supports
itself under and by pure contemptuous toleration or
cheery matter-of-courseness. Public worship requires
much care, much nurture: does it deserve all these
pains? Why, of course, *yes*, and YES again.

Then my dear friend Duchesne's death, on 21 April,
but known to me only on 30 April, gave me from
3 May to 17 May much, much trouble and some
anxiety in the study of his letters to me and the making
up of my mind what to insert in my letter to the
T.L.S., and how much to tell of the difficult matters
of debate which so largely filled his life and my feelings
and judgments. The thing was to have appeared this
week, but is now put off to next week—a truly difficult thing. But, mind, Dear, he was not "père"—
not a religious, but simply a secular priest, like
Abbé Huvelin. Then came the final settlements
with Mr. Thorold for his seeing my *Mystical Element*
through the press.

Then, on 17 May, tea with a sweet old, one-legged,
Jewish gentleman, full of woe as to the rampant
anti-Semitism of our day. A dear old thing; must
talk about him another time.

And then, 10–20 May, to Cambridge, with Aunt Mary, for my brother's honorary degree and garden-party. Hillie came down for the day.

My little old thing: this really must do for now. God bless you, and make you well, and help you to live, for these months, as much just simply for getting well as ever you can. I trust once at Peg Antrim's you will be in clover for these purposes. Drop, then, all else.

Loving old Uncle-Father,

F. v. H.

I send you nothing till you ask, indeed that is not important, nothing is, except what may help you to rest and to get well.

13 VICARAGE GATE

My darling Gwen-Child,   29 June, 1922.

This is the day of my first Holy Communion fifty-five years ago! So I *must* just write you a scrap at last! For *that* should be the very centre of a Christian's devotional life; to live up to *that*, no one can; but Christ can and will help, if only we are attentive and generous.

I really could not write these last—nearly three weeks, I fear it is. For I began with a very distinct nervous breakdown—such an old acquaintance that! Why, from eighteen to nearly thirty my life was pretty well blotted out by such troubles! They are very salutary for one, I find—they make one feel one's utter dependence upon God, even for getting away from utter self-absorption, which then seizes one all round. Nothing but dark rooms and much open air is then possible, but *that* is infallible as a gradual restorative—after a week or ten days.

Since then I have been in a condition of brainwork in the night, when deep points where I have been stuck for the last two years are getting wonderfully clear. But this also is very wearing, and also humbles one finely. I no more know how these lights are reached than I know how a penny in the slot should issue in a good, right railway ticket.

Two nights ago I had such absorbing pains of a kind I knew well—those which began the months of trouble which ended, twice, in big operations, that I went round yesterday to the surgeon that did them. But he found, for quite certain, that nothing of the kind was preparing, and that all the parts concerned are in perfect condition. That the pain was sciatica or rheumatism seizing hold of the old parts, because specially sensitive, I suppose, after all those happenings; this was a great relief to know, for otherwise my Giffords would have become uncertain.

Now, as to yourself, Child. I quite see the reason for your settling in London—it seems to me unanswerable, and that neither your love of the country nor H——'s dislike of such a move should deter you from it. After all, by getting high up and with some open space and greenery around you, it need not be emphatically towny.

I at once inquired of Mrs. Stuart-Moore, whom I now know well, and who has lived for years on the highest part here, in Campden Hill Square. Please, Dear, note carefully what she writes in the two notes enclosed. The second note is entirely about this matter. Pray specially note *what I have underlined in blue*, in the first note. You will see what a warm, kind soul she is! Don't want these back, second half of first note was too private to send on.

Hope to write about emotion soon.

How excellent Lundy Island sounds!

Loving,

Uncle-Father.

THURSLEY, NEAR GODALMING, SURREY

My ever darling Gwen-Child,   21 August, 1922.

What a wonderful place you have struck, for genuineness and always vital action and conviction! And yet there is also a further fact, to be deeply grateful for, that not only you yourself, but the three children too, possess tastes so direct and so genuine— so unspoilt by the "fine" world and by "good" society as to respond to it all and deeply to love it! Perhaps especially the letter of 18 August, received this morning, makes me feel this double gratitude for you, all four, very much indeed. Certainly, if such a place cannot keep people genuine, no place could!— You will be able to come back to it all every year, or at least often. But to live there entirely would hardly do, for any one of you four!

I am struck with what you say about church—of people, even there, not going into it to pray out of service times. My difficulty about this springs from the fact that with us Roman Catholics the frequentation of our churches at such times springs, I think, entirely

or all but entirely, from the Reserved Holy Eucharist,
and our Devotion to It. I doubt whether *we* have got
any more, or any very different, feeling, towards any
church or chapel of our own where (a rare thing)
there is no Reservation, than Protestants have towards
their churches out of service-times. Now, though the
Reservation of the Holy Eucharist is very old—we
can trace it back well into pre-Constantinian times—
yet the *Devotion* to the Reserved Holy Eucharist is
not older in England than about A.D. 1330, and,
I think, nowhere older than this anywhere. This is
curious, because the Reservation was always reverent,
and I know of no documents or facts to indicate that
the Catholics of all those centuries disbelieved in the
real Presence of Our Lord at such times—(the restriction of His Presence to the time between the conse-
cration and the communion is, I believe, a purely
Protestant notion). The Greek Russian Church, e.g.,
does not have it, but believes (and practises, or rather
has no active devotion) exactly as Western Christendom
believed and practised up to A.D. 1330 or so. What
happened to and in the Catholic churches up to about
1330? outside of service-times, I mean. I *think* there
must have been some praying there in between-whiles;
yet I doubt whether there was as much as since the
awakening of the Devotion to the Reserved Holy
Eucharist. It is this Devotion and Confessions of
Devotion which have largely built up the Roman
Catholic saints these last six centuries. Whereas devotion to the Holy Eucharist at Mass and Communion
only, and confessions of obligation, which built up the
Roman Catholic saints in the first thirteen centuries.

Am so glad to think you are coming to Vicarage

Gate in September. I am to be in Thursley myself (the address on this letter will alone be wanted) till 7 September for certain; but I am keeping myself open to stay on till 14 September or even 21 September (*at most*), in case health still requires it. Yet of course I much want to see you at home. Aunt Mary will certainly like to see you—to have you stay—the longer, the better.

Loving Uncle-Father,
F. v. H.

Three sets of books, October 1922. Two sets are for close study; the third set, a single book, is for lighter reading. Any one set can be studied, and the lighter book be read, at different times of the same day. But only one of the harder sets to be studied at the same time, and to be finished, before the second set is tackled.

I. *Three books* (four volumes) *on and of Aquinas.*

1. Philip Wicksteed on *The Reactions . . . St. Thomas Aquinas.*

A fine book by a lover of Aquinas. But Wicksteed is a Unitarian, and hence unperceptive as to *revealed* theology. Pray read twice, all the English parts (that is, only the lectures and *not* the *notes*), also the Preface (pages vii–xvi).

I would either omit Lecture III. (pages 157–196) and the second half of Lecture IV. (pages 260–78); or I would read it with aloofness and critical awakeness.

2. St. Thomas, *God and His Creatures.*

I would study all carefully, at least once. Pages 196–235 I would read and re-read, and copy out bits; glorious!

3. *Aquinas Ethicus*, two volumes.

I would read all at least once; and would carefully re-read and browse amongst the parts which specially help you. Be patient with your not understanding of much at first.

13 VICARAGE GATE, W.8

My darling Gwen-Child,   26 May, 1923.

Many thanks for prompt loan of this. Have taken all the particulars I wanted now; so here it is back.

There is one thing I much want you to undertake, and so to quiet me. *Promise you will instantly drop* EVERY WORD OF DANTE'S "INFERNO." I myself have never dared read more than scraps of it. Go to the *Paradiso*, and study this again and again. At first, each canto at least three times.

It would grieve me so if you get repelled by Dante, who otherwise could—and *will*—become part of your food and air—your daily food, your daily air.

I pray daily *specially* for what you told me of. God bless and brace and bear with us all!

> Loving old Fatherly Uncle,
>
> F. v. H.

Am mending; but still, bedroom for two or three more days.

13 VICARAGE GATE, KENSINGTON, W.8

My darling Gwen-Child,   11 July, 1923.

A matter goes revolving in my head about you, which, I think, I had better mention now, since you may be acting on it before we meet again next Monday. You told me you had promised—I did not catch whom —to read again ——'s last book; and indeed you took away my copy for the purpose. I have been feeling somewhat cross with anybody who would ask such a thing of you, since it doubtless means a wish that you may, after all, come to like the book, and you may then praise it, to the pleasure of all the author's family. And I think you could get yourself to do so, or at least to try. I care much for that family and wish them every consolation, yet I cannot doubt that we none of us ought—that we none of us have the right—to put this kind of pressure upon others. And to enter into such an affectionate little plot is, surely, not good for one's straightness—for that complete sincerity which alone gives value and the power to produce genuine pleasure to our literary judgments. But this point, too—I mean the moral point here involved—is for you to decide upon and follow, not for me to impose upon you. I only bring it up because you might acquire the habit before you had fully made up your mind.

And so that is *that*! It is simply for yourself, Child. Perfect simplicity, never forcing the note: this we will try and combine with kindliest reserve and softening judgments where we can. But *not* more. No court paid to families, etc.

Old Father,
F. v. H.

My darling Child,   22 October, 1923.

I loved getting your post card this morning—some
two hours ago, and hearing you had had so beautiful
a Retreat. Of course I am keenly looking forward to
seeing you when you are back, and when we can hit
off a day and time to fit us both—perhaps next Monday,
as before.

But I write because I want, if I can, promptly to
get quite clear in my old mind a matter that has been
a bit perplexing me. I have to take gas and have one
molar out this afternoon; and gas again and another
molar out some few days hence; and it will be joy
indeed, if I find that I was simply mistaken in the
following matter and learn this in between the two
little woes.

You see, my Sweet, you used to write to me often—
the oftener the better for me (provided the writing
came spontaneously to you, *without a touch of obligation
about it*). And I loved getting these letters and learnt
not a little from them, even though, latterly, I was
mostly too tired to answer by letter. And then you came
to Thursley, and I loved our time—I felt we had no
straining, etc., between us. You went off: well, and
thenceforward, somehow, the letters ceased. A pencil
note, merely as to health; then, quite shortly ago, a
joint little letter to Aunt Mary and me—this was all
during nine or ten weeks. But yesterday Hillie came
and, among other things about other people, told me
you had found me very tired at Thursley, and had
felt you ought not, then, to put any questions to me.
So I have come to think that probably you kept

silent, also as to letters, for my sake—to save me even the reading of them.

This morning's post card is so entirely the darling daughter, that I feel Hillie's report must be covering all. And so I feel I had better at once explain that *if you have not written as formerly* (I mean as to the quantity) *on my account*, I trust you will promptly drop any such notion and practice. Your letters simply rest and refresh me. But this, because they feel quite unforced, because I feel you to write them simply as the bird sings. And so, *if you have kept yourself from writing, even partly, because of yourself*—because it strained or hipped or otherwise tried you—*do not write as formerly till this feeling, if God wills, disappears*. It has been the fear that, by telling you all this, I might put pressure upon you, Child, that has kept me so long from saying anything. But when this Retreat of yours came and went without any account of it, I felt I must, somehow, find out. You are, Sweet, a humble soul, and may have thought I attached no importance to your letters. *If it was all for my sake*, you might now write me an account of the Retreat, still all fresh in your memory.

Ever loving Uncle-Father,

H.

13 VICARAGE GATE

My darling Child,   All Saints' Eve, 1923.

Here, for All Saints', is, at last, Elisabeth Leseur's *Journal* for you. Tried to get it ready-bound for you— but is not to be had like that; and I did not want to wait till I had got it bound for you—nowadays a long

process. I have got, at same time, a copy of my own—
so we can refer each other to anything we come upon
we like very much.

The three little books are simply the remaining
volumes of the Temple Dante, not yet taken home
by you. Mind you sometime read the *Monarchy* in the
Latin Works volume.

I loved getting your last *Zoo* and *National Gallery*
letter. We must talk about all in it on Monday next.

Have, at last, plunged again into my big book
composition, which I find turns into a prayer and
makes me very happy—was missing it greatly. But
this will make all mornings impossible to me for
anyone—even the child I am scribbling this to.

May we have a very, very deep and dear All Saints'
—the day of all the saints in all times and places and
disguises—so much the most of them known to God
alone; indeed the day also of the saintly bits, the
saintly moments, etc., the beginnings of sanctity in
souls, not otherwise saints at all.

God be with us.

> Your loving,
> Father.

13 VICARAGE GATE, W.8

My darling Child,   4 November, 1923.

Grateful thanks again, for the last interesting letters.
I could not answer your practical question—as to the
two hours taken by you in that church, at once; and
even now I can write only by doing so when I ought
not to do so—on Sunday, which works the full rest-
fulness for me only if I do not break in upon it at all.

I think your decision wise as far as its *interior* goes—that it will not strain you, accustomed and so happy as you are to and in long prayer. But is it wise *with your health* to tie yourself down thus to fixed days and hours? I wonder. 'Tis for you to watch how the arrangement works; and if the health really and clearly interferes with it, to give it up, I think.

As to to-morrow, Child, I shall love to see you, as always, and shall be sorry if you do not come, as always. But I feel as though it would be right for me not to accept your not coming *if your cold is still at a very fountainous stage*, since I am specially hopeful just now of avoiding grave, deep colds which would interfere with my resumed composition work—even perhaps my getting to our opening meeting of the L.S.S.R. at Mr. Montefiore's on Tuesday—day after to-morrow. But I trust your cold is getting fairly a *dry* one now, in which case, pray, pray, come, Sweet. In any case, mind to understand that the cold, in an acute condition, is the sole and complete objection to your coming.

I shall, otherwise, so greatly delight—over our hour after lunch here to-morrow.

I think Aunt Mary expects you fixedly already; if so, please telephone only if you are *not* coming.

Loving old Father-Uncle,

H.

Walter Frere, Bishop of Truro! Well, I hope and believe he will make a very good, because a supernaturally-minded, one.

How grand Elisabeth Leseur is—is she not?

H.

13 VICARAGE GATE

Darling Child,   17 March, 1924.

This is to dwell for a moment with you—in gratitude and deepest life-wishes for Olivia—seventeen to-day! Dear me! Clearly no more a child and yet, please God, with something of the child in her to the end! She is evidently an honourable, straight character, and God's grace and her own freely docile co-operation will slowly build up of all for something deep and tender.

And this wants, too, for a moment, to dwell upon your renouncing this Retreat. I wish now I had said nothing whatever in criticism of your going thus a third time a year to a Retreat. For it is difficult to see what precise harm there would be even in four such, provided they really brace and soothe you, the fact being that they are far more just times of escape from racket and to more prayer than usual. And again, I did and do see that having you at this Retreat would especially please Mrs. ——; and this too would be a pleasure surely not wrong, this although certainly such things ought primarily to be done because we ourselves require them. I do not propose your, after all, going, because to wobble up and down is never a good thing in itself; but if you have still left it half open and you still, at bottom, feel that *attrait* to it as just a (third) opportunity for more rest away, and prayer, then I incline not to abandon it, but quickly settle it up as a thing you are going to do.

I have written to Mrs. —— this morning, not about this, either way, but full of good will towards her, as indeed I ought to be.

Well, anyhow, to Thursday at one and two—much talk, Child.

Loving Fatherly One,

H.

13 VICARAGE GATE, KENSINGTON, W.8

12 August, 1924.

My darling Gwen-Child,   (Gertrude † 1915.)

I have been rather pursued by the fear that you might not get your cheque in time for such cashing of it as you may care to effect before leaving London on Thursday; and so, although I am looking forward (and much) to seeing you to-morrow (Wednesday), I am sending it enclosed to-night so as to reach you at home to-morrow (Wednesday, first post). I suppose you reach Hanover Terrace to-night; and, in any case, this letter will await you safely in your house. If you do arrive to-night, you can (if you like) cash the cheque in the morning to-morrow.

I also want to say that I have got St. Bernard's *Sermons on the Canticle of Canticles*, two volumes, for you. The volumes are stout but not large, so that I fancy you can easily take Volume I. to Lundy, if you like. It might be well to begin such a great new book out there.

I was so glad all went so well at that interview you feared so much in anticipation. I was very pleased to get that letter, and now the little one. But how nice to be talking together to-morrow.

Hillie is still away for a little Surrey visit; and Aunt Mary *may* be still away to-morrow. My chair takes

me out from three to five, and I have my tea at five.
Juliet Mansell has to be at her rehearsals till about
six-thirty. I should like you to arrive for your tea at
five, and to come down to me at five-thirty. Thus you
will see Aunt Mary or Hillie, if either of them is back;
and if you have to be alone—with Eva looking after
you! It will be for only half an hour.

Nothing in this letter wants an answer till you
answer me by word of mouth as to the cheque and
the book.

Loving Fatherly Uncle,

F. v. H.

13 VICARAGE GATE, KENSINGTON

Sunday, 14 September, 1924.

My darling Gwen-Child,

I find Professor Kemp Smith is right, who scolded
me for dictating him a long letter, for even that day
it markedly diminished the benefit of my rest. But this
is the last day of my holiday—I hope to begin work
anew to-morrow, although this persistent wet throughout more or less all the six weeks has much limited
the good derived from the rest. One long letter I could
not help writing—to Sir Archibald Geikie, whose auto-
biography has been the great delight of my holiday,
and who will be eighty-nine in December next—dear
warm heart, and pure, still very (mentally) active and
deeply religious life.

As to a Jowett's *Plato* for Richard, I am carefully
seeking a good, five-volume, copy—can well afford it
for Christmas. When I have got it, I shall give it to

you, for you to give to him. Say nothing of my intervention, please. I so love to think you say or imply literally *nothing* when (as so often) this is desirable. Hope Aunt Mary's letter has reached you; she told me she would write to you. Hillie has been staying with Beatrice Thynne.

Loving Uncle,
Freddy.